PAT'S SOURDOUGH
& FAVORITE RECIPES

PAT'S SOURDOUGH
&
FAVORITE RECIPES

by
PATRICIA A. DUNCAN

T.A.P. PUBLISHING CO.
P.O. Box 944
Douglas, Wyoming 82633

Library of Congress Number 89-90542

ISBN Number 0-9625098-1-7

1st Printing, 1990
2nd Printing, 1991

Printed in the Unites States of America
By
The CAXTON PRINTERS, Ltd.
Caldwell, Idaho 83605

DEDICATION

I dedicate this book to my husband Robbie because of his inspiration and patience while I was doing this book, and his love for sourdough. And to all the sourdough cooks in the world.

Table of Contents

ACKNOWLEDGMENTS

My thanks to John Baker, McCall, Idaho, for taking the picture for the cover.
To Jerry Antolik, Hudson, Wyoming, for the sketches and illustrations.
To Mike Cabral, Midwest, Wyoming, for the photograph of me on the back cover.

ABOUT SOURDOUGH

To Make Your Sourdough Starter

This is a very simple method and if cared for properly will work and keep forever.

3 small potatoes, peeled and
cut into four pieces
3 cups water
1 cake or envelope yeast (active)
½ tablespoon sugar
2 cups flour (more or less)
1 tablespoon sugar

Boil potatoes in 3 cups unsalted water until soft. Discard potatoes saving the potato water. Measure 2 cups of the potato water into a glass or pottery bowl and let cool to lukewarm. Mix in the yeast and ½ tablespoon sugar. Let stand until the yeast is working well. It will be light and frothy. Now add 2 cups flour and 1 tablespoon sugar. Mix well. Transfer to glass or pottery crock, cover with towel and let set in warm place for 3 days or until actively bubbling. It is important to stir the starter down each day. After the third day your starter is ready to use.

To replenish, add equal amounts of tepid water and flour. Store your starter in the refrigerator, uncovered.

Always mix up a sponge the night before you want to use your starter. To make the sponge: add equal amounts of flour and tepid water plus your start and 1 tablespoon sugar. Mix well. The amount of water and flour you will need will depend on the recipe you want to make. Always make up enough to set some back into the refrigerator for future use.

Three Day Sourdough Starter

1st day:
½ cup water
½ cup flour
1 tablespoon sugar

Mix well and set in a warm place and cover with a damp cloth.

2nd Day: 1 medium potato cut into small pieces and cooked in 1½ cups water. (No salt!)

Cool. When cool mash through a sieve. Add 1 cup of potato and water to the first days pot. Add ½ to ⅔ cup all purpose flour. Mix well. Cover and let set another day. Put any remaining potato and water in refrigerator for the third day.

3rd Day: Add remaining potato water to start. Add enough flour to make a sponge look to the start. Cover and let set for another day.

Your start should be ready to use on the fourth day. At night mix up your starter by adding 2 cups water, 2 cups flour and your start. Mix well. Add 1 tablespoon sugar. Mix well. Cover and let set overnight. Next morning take out enough start to keep in your refrigerator for future use. Always sprinkle a little sugar on top and set uncovered in your refrigerator, for your start needs air to work. Do not worry if there is a little water on top, just stir it back into the sponge.

What's left over is ready for you to make up into your favorite recipe.

Caring For Sourdough

Once your sourdough is started and working, it should always be kept in the refrigerator uncovered. Your sourdough needs air to grow. Always keep back enough starter to dip out some when you need it for biscuits and cakes. I always keep two separate jars of starter, one to dip from and the main Mother Reserve. When I make up my sponge for bread, I add both jars of starter to keep them fresh. If you dip out of your main starter jar, always add back the amount that you took out. If you took out one cup of starter, add 1 cup of water and 1 cup of flour, plus 1 teaspoon of sugar. Let stand at room temperature for at least 4 hours before setting back into the refrigerator. I always keep at least 3 cups of Mother Reserve back for future use.

Always keep your starter in a glass or crock jar. Always sprinkle the top with a small amount of sugar. *Do not use plastic or metal.* Your starter will pick up the taste of these products. You can mix up your sponge at night in a stainless steel bowl. But I do not suggest that you store your Mother Reserve in a stainless steel bowl.

If there is water on top of your starter, don't worry. Just fold it back into the starter. **DO NOT POUR IF OFF!** Sometimes there will be a crust on top. Just let the starter set at room temperature and the crust will dissolve back into your starter. You can scrape it off and discard it, but it is not necessary. Do not get salt into your starter. Salt will kill it! **DO NOT USE SELF-RISING FLOUR!**

Always remember to take your Mother Reserve back out of your sponge and return it to the refrigerator for future use.

I dry some of my starter just in case something should happen to the Mother Reserve, Heaven forbid! To dry the starter: When you make up a batch of sponge for bread, save out a cup or two. Add to this cup or two enough white or yellow cornmeal to make it stiff, but not too stiff. Spread the dough onto a floured surface and pat it down to 1/2-inch thick. Leave it to dry. When it is almost dry, cut into 1 inch squares, turn them over and continue to dry until very dry and firm. They should be dry enough to store in 24 hours. Put into an airtight jar and store in a dark, cool place. See Note:

To restart your starter from these dried cakes, crumble two or three of them into a cup of tepid water, add 1 tablespoon sugar. Let set for 12 hours or overnight in a warm place. When bubbly add 1 cup water, 1 cup flour and let set for another 12 hours. Now your starter is ready for use. I use it the first couple of times in hotcakes until the cornmeal is worked out. Just mix up enough sponge as you would for pancakes the night before. Take out enough to set back in the refrigerator to restart your Mother Reserve. Now you are back with a good spore, one that will work for you.

A GOOD SOURDOUGH STARTER IS CHERISHED AS MUCH AS GOLD. I know that mine is.

In caring for your starter, there are a lot of "Old Wives Tales," like, "You should never wash your starter crock." Not true. Your sourdough jars should be washed and rinsed thoroughly every time you mix up your sponge. If you do not use your starter once every week or two, dip out a cup and add a fresh cup of water and a cup of flour and a teaspoon of sugar. Mix it thoroughly and let set at room temperature for at least four hours. Return to refrigerator for future use. I call my starter my "Mother Reserve" and refer to it throughout the book as such.

Note: Your sponge may also be dehydrated by using your fruit trays that come with your dehydrater, spread out 1/2 cup of starter until it covers the tray. Repeat until you have enough starter to fill 4 or 5 trays or more. Turn dehydrater on and let dry until very dry, about 18 hours. When dry, put into a blender and blend until fine then put into an air-tight container. Your culture will keep for years this way.

To send for your dehydrated starter made from my 121 year old spore, please send your name and address, plus a $5.00 check or money order to:
Pat Duncan
P.O. Box 944
Douglas, Wyoming 82633

There are sourdough starters on the market. Just mix as directed on the package.

The secret to any good starter is plenty of use. Use it at least once every two weeks.

When baking breads you should know that different flours have different textures. So depending on the flour you use, you may have to add more flour than the recipe calls for or less flour than the recipe calls for. At sea level you would add more flour to get the texture of the sponge that you will need to make your bread. The only flour that I have used in the last 40 years is Gold Medal all-purpose flour. It works wonderful for me and I saw no reason to change.

Once you make a loaf of bread you will soon get the feel of how much flour to use. And once you start baking bread with your sourdough you will be hooked on a very special treat.

There are two important things to remember about cooking with sourdough.

1. Always mix up your start the night before or at least 6 hours before you intend to use a recipe.

2. Always read the recipe all the way through. You can do some substituting, such as margarine, for butter. But basically all recipes are made to be followed.

I received this letter from Jackie Smith, the daughter of Mrs. Myrtle Thrope, the lovely lady that gave me my start 43 years ago.

Dear Pat, Thank you so much for the cookbook. I thought it was very nice and when I had read Maude's copy, I figured the starter had been my Mom's. That Starter was a sacred thing in our house. When Mom had to be away from the ranch, all the ranch hands were schooled on how to take care of it until she returned. As a child we always had the large loaves of sourdough bread, all brown and crusty, and that wonderful aroma that greeted us as we arrived from school. Mom would allow me to cut the heals off and I would spoon on thick cream and sprinkle sugar on it and then was off to do the chores. (Kids had many chores in those days!)

Mom was born, Myrtle Inez Reed, on June 25th, 1898 in Tascasa, Texas, near the Canadian River, which is probably 40 miles from Amarillo.

The sourdough had been her Mothers, so have no idea how far it goes back — at any rate as a young woman (probably 17 years old) she traveled by covered wagon with her belongings to Cimarron County, Oklahoma. She married my dad in 1913 and we resided on that ranch until 1947. Dad died in 1929 and Mom ran the ranch and raised we kids alone. I was only 19 months old. We lived through the depression and the horrible "Dust Bowl Days!" In looking back, I know that only a very strong lady could have survived the hardship. Her cooking was legendary in our country, as was her cheerful nature. Mom was a practical nurse and she nursed far and wide and delivered many babies, as our closest Doctor was at Clayton, New Mexico, 50 miles away. Mom died in Ontario, Oregon in 1973 and is buried there. She never wanted to go back to Oklahoma, and always said, "THAT OLD WIND BLEW OVER ME ALL MY LIFE AND I CERTAINLY DON'T WANT IT BLOWING OVER ME WHEN I'M DEAD!"

How lucky we children were to have had such a wonderful Mom. Only after she was gone did I finally let the starter die. I'm glad someone has kept it alive.

Hope all is well with you and yours,

My Best,

Jackie Smith

My sourdough starter was given to me from a lady Rancher, Saddle Maker. She came from Texas and Oklahoma. She also said that her family had used it for over 80 years and that it traveled across the U.S. in a covered wagon. I can't vouch for her, but I can tell you that I have had her start for 40 years, making my start 120 years old. The more you use it the better it is. A housewife should at least once in her life, experience the joy of making homemade bread, sourdough or not. The aroma that fills the kitchen when the bread comes out of the oven is one that you will be proud of forever.

I am a person that uses her Mother Reserve (I will refer to the starter as Mother Reserve throughout the book) every week. We have sourdough biscuits at least once a week and always have sourdough bread on the table.

When I know that I will be away from home for more than 2 weeks, I take my starter with me. So far in my travels with my sourdough, I have left starts in at least 10 different states and Canada. My starter has made new friends in McCall, Idaho; South Dakota; Missoula, Montana; Tucson, and Ajo, Arizona; San Antonio, Texas; Midwest, Douglas, and Casper, Wyoming; Fairbanks and Petersburg, Alaska; California, Colorado and Oregon. I have traveled from California to Alaska and on to New York with it in my purse. From sea-level to a mile high, from humid climates to dry climates. I have never had a batch of bad bread. My sourdough always works for me. As a matter of fact it has never let me down! It is and always will be, one of my best friends. My traveling companion that never talks back!

Restaurants are very helpful when you need to work your start. Of course, they do want you to leave behind a starter for them when you leave. And I have done so many times.

One time when I was traveling from Wyoming to Oregon, I stopped at a service station for gas in Garden City, Idaho, and the owner of the station came out to help the attendant gas the car. He looked at me and then at the ice box on the floor of the front seat and said to the attendant, "I'll bet you ten dollars that this lady has a sourdough start and a bottle of red wine in that ice box." The bet was on, and of course, the attendant lost! It had been 10 years since I had seen the owner of that station. I guess he remembered me well.

I have given starts to Jim Moore at the Moore Ranch in Midwest, Wyoming, and to William I. Moore and William I. Moore, Jr., at the Hell and Back Ranch out of Douglas, Wyoming. All of these men do the sourdough cooking. God bless them. The Jim Moore family puts up with my cooking, whenever I show up at their ranch. My many thanks to them all. I have had many great experiences with my sourdough, and hope that all of you will have as many as I have had over the years.

Flynn Cabin

This Flynn Sheep Company cabin was built by Diamond L. Slim, "a tough old cowpoke" who always seemed to "hang around," and was the perpetrator of a "Wyoming Homestead Tragedy." After befriending a young couple named Church, he murdered them. He was later jailed and before he could stand trial, several cowboys from a nearby round-up formed a posse and broke Diamond L. from jail. They took him a short distance away to a railroad bridge, tied a hard twist rope around his neck and shoved him overboard. The jerk completely decapitated him. They left him there for the sheriff to find and rode secretly back to camp.

Diamond L. Slim was brought to justice in the style of the old west. An old sourdough yarn tells that his ghost still lingers on in the cabin and can be seen from time to time. After a drink or two!

The Flynn cabin is located on Antelope Creek in Northern Converse County, Wyoming, and belongs to The Hell and Back Ranch owned by William I. Moore, Jr. Mr. Moore has restored the cabin to its 1890 original state.

Diamond L. Slim's brand

My sourdough starter has now traveled, not only from the northern tip of Alaska, but to the northern tip of South America.

My husband Bob flew a C-46 for Haiti Air Freight International in Haiti. He flew from Haiti to Trinidad in the West Indies. Since I did not have a home to stay in in Haiti I flew every flight with him. What an adventure. The old engines would "POP" every once in awhile! But kept right on purring.

I carried my starter with me everywhere. I made fry-bread in Barbados. It tasted wonderful with flying fish. We had banana pancakes in San Juan. In Haiti, I just kept my starter safe and cold. Never had a problem with customs.

I was amazed at how the flours differed in each country. In the U.S. Virgin Islands the only flour you could find was in one pound packages. Since everything had to be shipped in by boat or plane, ready made bread was cheaper. Flour was very expensive. We flew bread all over the U.S. Virgin Islands, out of San Juan, Puerto Rico, in an old DC 3. We stayed a month in San Juan, Puerto Rico, and shared a four bedroom condo with three other couples. When I would get up and make sourdough biscuits for breakfast, the doors to rooms would open all of a sudden and the kitchen would become a "May I have one?" shop!

The texture of the flour would also differ from country to country. In Barbados the flour was more like the unrefined flour here in the states. Also a little brown in color. Some of the cooks in the restaurants would share their flour with me, in order to keep my starter going. Since bread was shipped in and flour a premium, most said, "It would be useless to keep a start for themselves." I gave a few starts to people for home use. I know they will enjoy it.

Life in Haiti was very uneasy. I carried a camera out on the street one day and was chased. Because of voodoo religion, Haitians do not like to be measured. Taking a picture would have measured them. I was forbidden to go in the street with my camera. We stayed two blocks from Papa Doc's Castle, and I did get some great snapshots of the Castle. Out walking one day, a young school girl stopped me and reached up and touched me on the cheek. She had never seen an American before.

Most of the people are very poor. I wished that I could bake all the bread in the world and give it away, to some of the poor starving people that we saw in Haiti. When it rained you would see all sorts of naked boys and girls, bathing in the ponds that filled with the rain water. My heart went out to them. For us to live in such a free country as we do in America, it is sad to see so much suffering in Haiti, and yet the people were so proud!

The smell of fresh, hot bread from the oven often brings back the wonderful memory of two hobos who used to make frequent visits to my grandmother Lloyd's ranch in St. Onge, South Dakota.

Her ranch was only about half a mile from the railroad tracks. In the late 1930s the hobos would smell the fresh bread (I'd swear) and come knocking at the door. The same ones would always return. I can remember how they would tease me by saying one was Bo and other one was Ho.

Grandmother would hand out slices of bread with honey to them and any leftover stew. She would latch the screen and chat to them about whether or not the leaves had changed colors yet in Iowa or how is the weather in Ohio? It was like taking a trip she could not afford.

I was there when they arrived one day. Ho was dressed in a tattered and torn red plaid mackinaw jacket. But "clean shaven" he was. Wanting grandmother to be impressed, to be sure.

Bo was in farmer's overalls and heavy boots. He had a beard and deep wrinkles in his face. A very well spoken man he was. Grandmother said, "He was at one time a Boston lawyer whose wife ran off with the town banker." He hopped the rails to shame her and being a bum became his new way of life.

Grandmother's bread was well known to the bums who rode the stretch of rail the Old Galloping Goose traveled across South Dakota in the thirties.

It was a hot draught summer in the middle of August 1934, the sounds of the Gypsy Bells were heard coming from down the dry country road. One old used up mare, with a collar of bells, ringing out a jingle that could be heard for a mile around.

We children ran to Mother yelling, "the gypsy wagons are coming, the gypsies are coming!" Mother at once sent us to the back yard.

Every year the colorful group of wagons and people would come. The ladies wore long bright dresses and wore bandanna's, of all different colors wrapped around their heads. This was a year that we had not had anything to give away, due to the long hot summer and no rain. Mother would have to forgo the fabric and beads, that she use to trade for. As she was telling this very thing to the old lady at the front door, the other gypsies were going to the water tank to fill their jugs and to water the horses, on the way they heard that there was not to be any food at this stop and saw the young girl playing in the yard. One large lady ran and grabbed the little girl and headed off to the wagon. She tossed a shawl over my head so that no one could hear me cry, and quickly all the wagons left to go on down the road. It was almost an hour later that I was found to be missing! Mother quickly ran for Dad and together they grabbed a couple of old laying hens, a bucket of potatoes and some flour from the bin, a loaf of home-made bread, and the "shotgun," and Dad was off on the tractor to chase down the wagons! The rescue mission was quick. There was no fuss when he caught up with the caravan. It seemed that the old lady was "Damn" glad to get rid of the kicking, screaming, biting little freckled face girl. After all, all they wanted was food, and now were happy.

Man was I ever glad to see Father! And glad that I did not have to live with that awful smelling lady.

Sourdough Bagels, Onion and Garlic

4 cups sourdough starter
1 cup milk, heated to lukewarm
¼ cup butter, melted
3 tablespoons onion, chopped fine
2 large cloves garlic, chopped fine
1 teaspoon salt
5 cups flour

Set your starter the night before, using 3 cups water, 3 cups flour and your Mother Reserve, add 1 tablespoon sugar. Mix well, cover and let set overnight. Next morning take your Mother Reserve back out and cover with a small amount of sugar and return uncovered to the refrigerator.

Measure out 4 cups of starter to use for the bagels. Warm milk until the chill is off or until lukewarm. Melt the butter. Add milk and butter to starter. Add the chopped onions and garlic. (Be sure the onions and garlic are chopped very fine.) Add the salt and 4 cups of the flour. Mix thoroughly, turn out onto floured board or canvas on which the other cup of flour has been added. Knead until smooth, about 10 minutes. Put into a greased bowl to let rise until double in size.

Punch down and divide into equal pieces. Roll each piece into a rope 7 inches long and taper at the ends. Wet the ends to help seal into a circle. Let rise, covered on a floured board for at least 15 to 20 minutes. Drop the rings into a solution of: 2 quarts of boiling water and 1 tablespoon sugar. Drop them in one or two at a time. As bagels surface, turn them over and cook for another 3 minutes. Skim out and place on an ungreased baking sheet. Coat with **beaten egg white.** Bake in a preheated oven 400° F for 20 to 25 minutes.

Serve with cream cheese or toasted with butter. Makes 24 bagels.

Sourdough Applesauce Nut Bread

2½ cups flour
3 teaspoons baking powder
1 teaspoon salt
½ teaspoon cinnamon
¾ cup sugar
1 cup chopped nut meats
2 eggs, well beaten
1 cup applesauce
½ cup sourdough starter
2 tablespoons melted butter
½ cup raisins (can be omitted)

Beat eggs. Add applesauce and melted butter. Add sourdough starter. Add sugar and beat well. Now add all the dry ingredients, nuts, raisins and beat well. Bake in a greased and floured loaf pan at 350° F for 1 hour.

Sourdough Banana Nut Bread

1 cup sugar
⅓ cup Crisco oil
2 eggs, beaten
½ cup sourdough starter
2 cups flour, all-purpose, unsifted
1 teaspoon salt
1 teaspoon soda
3 ripe bananas, crushed
¾ cup chopped nuts
1 teaspoon vanilla

Mix sugar and Crisco oil together. Beat in eggs. Fold in sourdough starter. Add the rest of the ingredients. Bake in a loaf pan in center of oven, preheated at 375° F for 40 to 50 minutes or until done. Be sure to grease and flour the loaf pan before adding the batter. Bread is done when inserting a toothpick and it comes out clean. Turn out onto wire rack to cool.

Sourdough makes this a nice, moist banana bread that is a pleasure to eat and serve.

Sourdough Bannock and Beans

BANNOCK

1 cup cornmeal
1 cup regular or quick oatmeal
1 cup buttermilk
2 tablespoons melted butter
2 tablespoons honey
½ teaspoon ginger
½ cup sourdough starter
1 teaspoon soda

Mix all ingredients together in order given. Grease a heavy skillet with bacon drippings. Pour the batter into the hot, greased pan and cook on top of the stove at medium heat for 10 minutes. Transfer skillet to preheated oven 375° F for an additional 20 minutes. Cut into wedges and serve hot.

Note: Bacon bits or leftover beef, onions, peppers or any type of vegetables may be added to Bannock.

BEANS

No exact amounts of anything are required in this recipe.

Wash and pick over 1 or 2 pounds of small white beans. If desired let set overnight with enough water to cover and 2 teaspoons soda. Rinse and cover with water and bring to a boil. Drain again. Now the beans are ready to cook. Add beef bouillon to cover the beans. Return the beans to the stove to cook. Add 1 sliced carrot, 1 diced onion, ¼ pound diced salt pork or ham. The beans will swell considerably when they cook, so you may need to add more water or broth. Salt and pepper to taste.

Serve with Bannock.

Sourdough Bread Sticks

This recipe is for garlic sticks.

⅓ cup of olive oil
6 cloves garlic, minced
1 tablespoon sugar
Salt to taste
Melted butter, ⅓ cup
2 cups sourdough sponge
3 cups flour

Take your Mother Reserve starter from the refrigerator the night before. Mix with 2 cups tepid water and 2 cups flour. Cover and let set overnight. Next morning take your Mother Reserve out and return it to the refrigerator. In the leftover sponge, mix the 4 minced garlic cloves, the sugar and 2 tablespoons of the melted butter. Mix in enough flour to make the dough elastic and smooth, about 2 to 3 cups. Knead until very smooth. Put into a greased bowl and let rise until double in size. Now divide into 12 equal parts and roll into ropes. Cut into 12-inch long ropes and roll in the olive oil that you have added the other 2 minced cloves of garlic to. The garlic cloves should be put into the olive oil and be blending while the bread dough is rising. After the ropes have been rolled into the oil, place them onto a cookie sheet that has been greased with the remaining garlic oil. Cover and let stand until puffy looking. Brush with melted butter and cook in a preheated oven at 400° F for 20 minutes. Remove and brush again with any leftover garlic oil mixture. Remove to racks and cool.

CHEDDAR CHEESE BREAD STICKS

Omit garlic and add 1 cup grated Cheddar cheese.

DILL BREAD STICKS

Add 1 tablespoon of dill weed into the bread mixture and omit the garlic.

Sourdough Boston Brown Bread

Set oven at 350° F.

1 tablespoon molasses
2 cups raisins or currants
2 cups cold water
1 cup sourdough starter
2 teaspoons soda — pinch of salt
1 cups sugar
2¾ cups flour
2½ tablespoons butter, melted
1 egg
1 teaspoon vanilla
1 cup nutmeats, chopped

Mix molasses, raisins, water, cook together for 15 minutes. Cool. Add soda and mix. Add sugar, sourdough starter, salt, vanilla, egg, and melted butter. Mix thoroughly. Add flour and mix. Stir in nutmeats. Bake in greased pans or #2 cans in 350° F for 1 hour.

Sourdough Buttermilk Corn Sticks

Vegetable oil
1 cup yellow cornmeal
¼ cup sourdough starter
1 teaspoon soda
½ teaspoon salt
1¾ cups buttermilk
1 egg, slightly beaten
4 teaspoons butter, melted

Preheat oven to very hot; 450° F. Brush heavy cast iron corn stick pan with vegetable oil. Place pan in oven while oven is heating to temperature, just until they are hot.

Combine cornmeal, baking soda, and salt in a medium-sized bowl. Stir in buttermilk, egg, sourdough starter and melted butter until well blended. Remove heated corn stick pans from oven; pour in cornmeal batter, filling about ⅔ full. Bake in preheated oven 450° F for 10 minutes until corn sticks are browned and have pulled away from sides of pan. Remove corn sticks. Serve warm.

Sourdough Cinnamon Drop Coffee Cake

2 cups starter sponge (see Note)
1 tablespoon honey
½ teaspoon salt
3 tablespoons melted butter
2½ to 3 cups flour

Mix butter (melted), salt and honey into starter. Add flour and work until blended. Turn out onto floured board and knead until smooth and elastic. Put into a greased bowl and cover with a damp towel. Let rise until double in size.

Have ready:

1 cup melted butter
1 cup white granulated sugar
1 cup brown sugar
4 tablespoons cinnamon
½ cup raisins
½ cup chopped walnuts

When the dough has doubled in size, melt the butter. Set aside. In a separate bowl mix the brown and white sugar together with the 4 tablespoons of cinnamon. Have the raisins and walnuts ready on the side.

Now grease a tube angel cake pan with butter.

Break or cut off large walnut size chunks of dough and drop them into the melted butter, then roll the chunks into the sugar mixture, making sure they are well coated. Then drop them into the pan. When the bottom has been covered with chunks, sprinkle the top of them with raisins and some of the walnuts. Continue to layer the chunks until the pan is over half full. Layer the chunks, buttered and sugared, sprinkled with raisins and nuts, until finished. Cover and let rise until double in size. Cook in a 375° F oven for 45 minutes or until done.

Note: Take your Mother Reserve out of the refrigerator the night before. Mix with 2 cups water, 2 cups flour and 1 tablespoon sugar. Cover. Let set overnight. Next morning put Mother Reserve back into refrigerator. Use rest of starter to make cinnamon cake.

Sourdough Cinnamon Raisin Bread

2 cups sourdough starter sponge
(see Note)
3 tablespoons sugar
1 teaspoon salt
2 tablespoons melted butter
3 cups Gold Medal flour
1 cups raisins
¼ cup sugar, 2 tablespoons cinnamon
2 tablespoons water
Butter, softened

To the sourdough starter, add 3 tablespoons sugar, salt, and melted butter. Beat until smooth. Add raisins and 3 cups of flour. Work until smooth and elastic. More flour can be added as needed. Turn out onto a floured board and knead until smooth and easy to handle. Place into a greased bowl; greased side up, cover with a damp cloth and let rise until double in size. Punch down dough; divide into halves. Roll each half into rectangle, 18x9 inches. Mix the ¼ cup sugar and the cinnamon. Sprinkle each half with 1 tablespoon water and half of the sugar mixture. Roll up beginning at the 9-inch side of hand, press each end to seal; fold ends under. Place seam side down in greased loaf pan, 9x5x3 or 8½x4½x2½ inches. Brush lightly with butter. Let rise until double in size. About 1 hour.

Heat oven to 425° F. Bake until deep, golden brown and loaves sound hollow when tapped; 30 to 35 minutes. Brush loaves with butter. Cool on wire rack. Makes 2 loaves.

Note: Take Mother Reserve from refrigerator the night before.

Mix with 2 cups water, 2 cups flour and the Reserve starter. Beat well. Cover and let set overnight. Next morning be sure to return your Mother Reserve to the refrigerator for future use.

Sourdough Cinnamon Tea Bread

1½ cups sourdough starter: Mix the starter the night before by adding 1½ cups water, your Mother reserve and 1½ cups flour plus 1 tablespoon sugar. Next morning take your reserve back out and return to the refrigerator for future use.

To the remaining 1½ cups starter add:

½ cup sugar
1 teaspoon salt
2 beaten eggs
¼ cup melted butter
½ cup milk
2½ cups all purpose
gold medal flour

Mix sourdough starter, sugar, salt and eggs with melted butter and milk. Stir in flour one cup at a time. Use more flour if needed – whatever it takes to make a stiff dough. Knead on a floured board for 10 minutes. Put into a greased bowl, turn over to get grease on top. Cover and let rise until double in size.

Roll dough to ½-inch thick. Brush with ¼ cup melted butter. Sprinkle with ½ cup sugar that has been mixed with 1½ tablespoons cinnamon. Roll as for jelly roll. Bake in a loaf pan or on a cookie sheet.

Makes two loaves. Bake 45 minutes at 375° F.

Sourdough Cornbread

1 cup starter
1½ cups yellow cornmeal
1½ cups evaporated milk
2 eggs, beaten
2 tablespoons sugar
¼ cup melted butter
½ teaspoon salt
¾ teaspoon soda

Thoroughly mix starter, cornmeal, milk, eggs and sugar in a large bowl. Stir in melted butter, salt and soda. Turn into a 10-inch greased fry pan.

Bake at 450° for 25 to 30 minutes.

Sourdough Cornbread

1 egg, well beaten
1 cup milk
2 tablespoons melted
shortening or butter
1 cup sifted flour
1 cup yellow cornmeal
1 tablespoon sugar
1 teaspoon salt
1 cup sourdough starter
2 teaspoons baking powder

Mix all ingredients until just blended. Pour into greased 8x8-inch pan. Bake 25 minutes at 350°.

Sourdough Southern Cornbread

¼ cup shortening
2 cups white cornmeal
3 tablespoons flour
2 teaspoons baking powder
1 teaspoon soda
½ cup sourdough starter sponge
1 teaspoon salt
1 egg
2 cups buttermilk

Melt shortening in a 9-inch square baking dish in oven, brushing sides of pan with melted shortening.

Sift together dry ingredients. Combine egg, buttermilk and sourdough. Stir into dry ingredients along with melted shortening. Pour batter into hot pan. Bake in 450° oven for 20 to 25 minutes.

This is very good with added bacon bits.

Sourdough Yankee Skillet Cornbread

1¼ cups sifted flour
¾ cup yellow cornmeal
2 tablespoons sugar
4 teaspoons baking powder
1 teaspoon salt
1 egg
1 cup sourdough starter
⅔ cup milk
⅓ cup shortening, melted

Sift flour, cornmeal, sugar, baking powder and salt. Stir in milk, sourdough starter, melted shortening and beaten egg. Stir just until blended. Pour into 8 inch skillet, well greased. Bake in 425° oven for 30 minutes.

This recipe may be doubled for more volume.

Rich Sourdough Cornbread

1½ cups yellow cornmeal
1 cup all-purpose Gold Medal Flour
⅓ cup sugar
1 teaspoon salt
1 tablespoon baking powder
½ cup sourdough starter
2 eggs
6 tablespoons melted butter
8 tablespoons melted and
    slightly cooled shortening
1½ cups milk

Preheat oven to 400° F. Sift into a mixing bowl the cornmeal, flour, sugar, salt and baking powder. Beat eggs, add the butter, shortening and sourdough. Stir in the milk. Mix in the dry ingredients and beat very lightly until all the flour is moist. Pour into an 8x8-inch buttered baking dish and bake in center of oven for 30 minutes. Serve hot.

Mexican Sourdough Cornbread

1 cup sourdough
1 cup Albers yellow cornmeal
1 cup flour
t tablespoon baking powder
1 teaspoon salt
1 egg
1 cup milk
1 cup cream style corn or fresh
    corn scrapped from the cob
¼ cup finely chopped onion
2 finely chopped fresh
    jalapeno peppers
¼ cup butter, melted
½ cup shredded cheddar cheese

Beat egg and milk together, add starter, corn and melted butter. Add onion, jalapenos, cheddar cheese and all dry ingredients. Stir until just blended. Pour into well-buttered 8x8-inch square pan. Bake in hot oven (400° F.) 35 to 40 minutes.

Sourdough Dill Bread or Dinner Rolls

3 cups starter sponge
    (mixed up the night before)
¾ teaspoon salt
2 tablespoons butter, melted
2 tablespoons dillweed
2 cups flour, plus
    enough on board to knead

The night before mix 2 cups water, 2 cups flour, 1 tablespoon sugar and your Mother Reserve. Cover and let set overnight. Next morning take your reserve starter back out, cover with a dash of sugar and return to refrigerator for future use.

Mix the 2 tablespoons melted butter, salt and dillweed into the starter that is left. Work in enough flour to make a stiff dough. Turn onto a floured board and knead for 300 strokes. Turn into a greased bowl, turn to get grease on top, cover and let rise until double in size. Turn out and punch down. Make into 2 small loaves or pinch off balls and roll in palm of hand into round balls. Put into an 8x8-inch pan. Let rise again until double in size. Bake at 375° F. for 35 to 40 minutes.

Sourdough Date Bread

1 package dates, cut fine
2 teaspoons soda
2 tablespoons butter
1½ cups boiling water
    (you may substitute ½ cup rum
    for the ½ cup of water)
2 cups sugar
2 eggs
1 cup sourdough starter
3 cups flour
1 cup chopped nuts
¼ teaspoon salt
¼ tablespoon vanilla

Mix dates, (chopped fine), soda, butter and water. Allow to cool. Then add sugar, eggs, sourdough, flour, nuts, salt and vanilla. Pour into 3 greased and floured loaf pans. Bake for 1¼ hour in a slow oven, 275° F.

Egg Nog Sourdough Bread

Bread:
4 cups sourdough starter sponge
2 tablespoons honey
1½ teaspoons cream of tartar
1 teaspoon salt
4 cups all-purpose flour
3 eggs
2 tablespoons melted butter or oleo
½ teaspoon nutmeg
1 teaspoon vanilla or rum extract

Set your starter the night before by adding your sourdough start to 2½ cups water and 2½ cups all-purpose flour. Mix well. Sprinkle top with 1 teaspoon sugar. Cover and let set overnight. Next morning take your Mother Reserve back out and return to the refrigerator for future use.

To the 4 cups of starter sponge add the eggs and beat well. Add the melted butter, honey and vanilla. Stir until blended. Mix flour, salt, cream of tartar and nutmeg. Add to sponge a cup at a time. Knead until smooth. About 10 minutes. Put into a glass bowl that has been greased, turn once to get oil on both sides. Cover with a damp cloth and let rise until double in size. Beat down with fists and make into loaves. Put into 2 loaf pans, let raise again until double in size. Bake for 50 minutes at 375° F. or until done. Makes 2 loaves or 30 dinner rolls.

Goes wonderfully with Thanksgiving Dinner. Makes great turkey sandwiches.

Sourdough Dresden-Style German Stollen

⅓ cup finely chopped candied orange peel
½ cup golden raisins
½ cup seedless raisins
½ cup currants
½ cup slivered almonds
1 egg white beaten with 1 teaspoon water
¼ cup melted butter
⅓ cup powdered sugar
½ cup milk
1 cup butter
½ cup sugar
2 cups sourdough starter sponge (see note)
½ teaspoon salt
1 teaspoon almond flavoring
1 teaspoon grated lemon peel
5 cups all purpose flour, unsifted (more or less)
2 eggs

In a small pan combine milk, butter and sugar. Place over medium heat and bring mixture to scalding, stirring to dissolve the sugar. Set aside to cool. Beat the eggs into the cooled egg mixture. Add this mixture to the 2 cups of sourdough starter, beat until well blended. Add salt, almond flavoring, lemon peel and 3 cups of the flour. Mix until well-blended. Stir in orange peel, raisins, currants and almonds. Add enough flour to knead. Turn out onto a floured board and knead until smooth and elastic. About 10 minutes. Turn dough over in a greased bowl. Cover and let rise in a warm place until double in size. Punch dough down; divide in half. On a lightly greased baking sheet shape the dough, each half, into a 7x9-inch oval, about 1 inch thick. Brush the surface with some of the egg-white mixture, then crease ovals and fold them lengthwise, but not all the way over leaving a 2-inch lap on bottom. Brush top with egg-white mixture. Cover and let rise until double in size. Bake in 375° F. oven for 40 minutes or until richly browned. Brush top with melted butter and sift the powdered sugar over top. Return Sollens to oven and bake 3 minutes longer to set sugar. Cool on wire racks.

Make several and give as Christmas gifts.

Sourdough Mexican Spoon Bread

1 can cream style corn
1 cup yellow cornmeal
¾ cup buttermilk
½ teaspoon soda
½ cup starter
⅓ cup oil
1 teaspoon salt
2 eggs

Mix all top ingredients together well. Melt 1 tablespoon butter in casserole. Add ½ of the batter.

Place 1 can chopped green chilie's over batter. Cover with 1½ cups grated cheddar cheese. Pour balance of batter over cheese.

Bake in hot oven 450° F. for 30 minutes.

Sourdough Navajo Fry Bread

4 cups flour
1 tablespoon baking powder
1 teaspoon salt
2 tablespoons melted butter
2 cups milk
1 cup sourdough
starter sponge
cooking oil

Sift flour with the baking powder and salt into a large bowl. Add melted butter, milk and sourdough starter a little at a time, mixing by hand until dough is soft. Knead dough on a lightly floured board until dough has absorbed all flour. Pat dough into flat, round cakes about 5 inches in diameter and ¼ to ½ inch thick. Pour ¼ inch oil into a large heavy skillet. Heat oil and brown patty quickly, one at a time, until golden brown on both sides. Cut into wedges and serve with jams or just eat with butter.

This recipe keeps well up to a week or so in the refrigerator. Break off pieces and fry for any meal.

Jalapeno Cheddar Cheese Bread

3 cups sourdough starter sponge
¾ teaspoon salt
2 tablespoons butter, melted
½ cup chopped fresh jalapeno
peppers, seeds and skins
1 cup grated cheddar cheese
2 cups all-purpose flour

Mix starter the night before by adding starter to 2 cups flour, 2 cups water and 1 tablespoon sugar. Mix well. Cover and let set overnight. Next morning put Mother Reserve back into refrigerator. Mix salt, butter, jalapenos and cheddar cheese into the leftover starter. Mix in enough flour to make a stiff and workable dough. Turn out onto a floured surface and knead until smooth and elastic. Put into a greased bowl and let rise until double in size. Make into dinner rolls and put into an 8x8-inch greased pan. Let rise again until double in size. Bake in 375° F. oven for 40 minutes.

Sourdough French Bread

The night before, take your Mother Reserve out of the refrigerator and mix with 4 cups water, 4 cups flour (I use all-purpose Gold Medal Flour) and 1 tablespoon sugar. Mix well. Cover and let set overnight. Next morning take out your Mother Reserve and cover lightly with sugar (about 1 teaspoon) and set uncovered in the refrigerator until future use.

In the starter sponge that is left in the bowl, mix 3 tablespoons of melted butter, 1½ teaspoons salt or more to taste and 5 cups flour. Mix until hard to work in bowl. Put another cup of flour onto a board or canvas and work or knead for at least 300 strokes. Your bread should be very elastic and smooth. As my grandmother used to say, "as smooth as a baby's butt". Put into a well-greased bowl and cover with a damp cloth and let rise until double in size. Punch down and make into loaves. Let rise again until double in size. Brush top with cold water. Cook in a 375° F. oven for 50 minutes. This will make three loaves. Round or medium size bread pans.

This is the basic Sourdough Bread recipe. From here you can add or subtract from the amount of water in the sponge at night. Your flour and water will almost always equal the same. Such as 2 cups of water, 2 cups of flour, tablespoon sugar and your Mother Reserve will make a smaller amount of bread. Always remember to take your Mother Reserve out before adding salt! Salt will kill your starter. Also be sure that you DO NOT USE SELF-RISING FLOUR!

If you like more holes in your Sourdough French bread you may add a package of yeast. Dissolve as directed on package and add to sponge after Mother Reserve has been taken out. Continue recipe. If loaves are made into rounds, split tops with a sharp knife before putting into oven. Three lines across the top or criss-cross on top. Rain or shine I have never had a bad loaf of Sourdough Bread.

Sourdough Nepalese Bread

1½ cup sourdough
starter sponge (see note)
2 cups whole wheat flour
2 tablespoons sugar
½ teaspoon baking powder
½ teaspoon salt
¼ teaspoon cinnamon
¼ teaspoon nutmeg
¼ teaspoon cloves
1 egg, slightly beaten
½ cup milk

In sourdough starter put the beaten egg and the ½ cup milk. Sift all the dry ingredients together; add to the starter mixture. Work until the dough forms a smooth ball. Add more flour if needed. Dough should not be sticky, but should be soft. Cover and let rise for ½ hour or so. Divide into 4 equal parts. Shape each into a ball. On a lightly floured board, roll out each ball into an 8-inch circle. Cut into quarters. Heat 1½ inches of salad oil in a heavy skillet at 400°. Lower one portion of dough at a time into hot oil; as soon as it returns to the surface, immediately turn over, using a slotted spatula. Continue to cook for 2 minutes or until puffed and golden brown. Lift out and drain on paper towels. Serve warm. Goes very good with lamb stew.

Note: Take your Mother Reserve out of refrigerator the night before, mix 1½ cups water, 1½ cups flour and the Mother Reserve and 1 tablespoon sugar. Cover and let set overnight. Next morning take your Mother Reserve back out, cover with dash of sugar and return to the refrigerator for future use.

Sourdough Norwegian Holiday Bread

The night before set starter by putting 2 cups water, 2 cups flour, add your Mother Reserve and 1 tablespoon sugar. Mix well and cover with a damp cloth and let set overnight. Next morning take out your Mother Reserve and return it to the refrigerator.

With the dough that is left add:

Heat ½ cup butter with ½ cup milk until the butter is melted. Cool until lukewarm. When cool add to the starter mixture. Then add 1 teaspoon salt, ¼ cup sugar, ½ cup candied cherries, ½ cup pineapple and 1 cup raisins and chopped nuts (if desired). Mix well. Now gradually add 3½ cups flour. More if needed to form a stiff dough. Knead well. Let rise in a warm place until double in size (1 to 2 hours). Turn out and shape as follows: Divide into 2 or 3 equal parts in round loaves. Place on a greased cookie sheet and let rise until light and double in size. About 1 hour. Bake 40 to 45 minutes at 375° F. Brush with egg white if desired. Frost with a light butter and powder sugar frosting. Decorate with candied cherries.

Oatmeal Raisin Cinnamon Bread

Makes 2 medium loaves.

Preparation: Set start the night before. Add 2½ cups water, 2½ cups flour and your Mother Reserve. Mix well and cover and let set overnight. Next morning take enough reserve back out for future use. Return it to the refrigerator. Take 4 cups of regular oatmeal and grind in your blender until super fine (or use a Vita Mix to grind oatmeal into flour). Makes 2¾ cups of oat flour. Grease 2 Pyrex bread pans, 8x4½x2½.

Recipe:

4 cups sourdough starter sponge
3 cups all-purpose flour
1 teaspoon salt

1 cup raisins
2 teaspoons cinnamon
2¾ cups oat flour
1 cup whole wheat flour
3 tablespoons melted butter or Crisco

Add the raisins, salt and melted butter to the 4 cups of starter. Mix well. Add oat flour and cinnamon. Mix well. Add the whole wheat flour and 2 cups of the all-purpose flour. Knead. Put the last cup of flour onto a board and turn the bread out and knead until smooth and elastic. More flour may be added if needed. Put into greased bowl, turn once to get grease on both sides. Cover with a damp cloth. Let raise until double in size, at least one hour. Punch down and form into 2 loaves. Put into greased pans and cover and let raise until double in size. Cook in a pre-heated oven 375° F. for 50 minutes. Put onto cooling rack. Brush tops with melted butter.

Spicy Pumpkin Bread

1 16 ounce can pumpkin
1½ sticks of butter
1½ cups sugar
4 eggs
⅔ cup milk (or ⅔ cup
fresh squeezed orange juice)
½ cup sourdough starter
3 tablespoons molasses
3½ cups Gold Medal flour
2 teaspoons soda
1 teaspoon salt
1 teaspoon cinnamon
1 teaspoon cloves
½ teaspoon nutmeg
⅔ cup nuts, chopped
⅔ cup raisins (optional)

Heat oven to 350° F. Grease and flour two 9x5x3-inch loaf pans.

In a large bowl cream butter, sugar and molasses until light and fluffy. Stir in the eggs, pumpkin and milk or orange juice. Beat until light and fluffy. Mix in sourdough starter. Now add all the other ingredients. Stir in nuts and raisins. Pour into pans. Bake about 70 minutes or until done when a toothpick inserted comes out clean.

Sourdough Pumpkin Loaf

4 eggs
2 cups sugar
1 cup salad oil
1 15 ounce can pumpkin
2 cups flour
1 tablespoon baking powder
1 cup sourdough starter
1 teaspoon cinnamon
½ teaspoon allspice
½ teaspoon nutmeg
1 tablespoon soda
1 cup chopped nuts

Beat eggs, add sugar, oil, pumpkin and sourdough starter. Combine dry ingredients and add to pumpkin mixture. Add nuts. Place in two greased loaf pans. Bake for 1 hour at 350°.

Molasses Sourdough Pumpernickel Bread

For those who really like Pumpernickel Bread this is one really nice Rich recipe. With the rye, whole-bran and molasses it is fine in texture and sweet. Very good with sliced cheese.

2 tablespoons butter
2 cups milk
1½ teaspoons salt
½ cup dark molasses
2 cups sourdough starter
  (see note)
⅓ cup firmly packed brown sugar
1½ cups whole-bran cereal
4 cups medium grind rye flour
5½ cups all-purpose flour
1 egg yolk mixed with
  1 tablespoon water

In a pan melt the butter, stir in the milk, salt and molasses. Add the 2 cups of sourdough starter sponge, bran-cereal, rye flour and 2 cups of the all-purpose flour. Beat until very well blended. Now work in the rest of the flour as needed to knead the dough until smooth and elastic. Turn out onto a lightly floured board and knead for about 10 minutes. Put into a well-greased bowl, cover and let rise until double in size. Punch down dough. Grease a couple of cookie sheets. Make dough into 3 round loaves. Flatten them slightly. Let rise again until double in size. With a sharp knife cut ½-inch slashes on top of each loaf. Brush with the egg yolk mixture.

Bake in a 350° F. oven for 40 minutes or until golden brown.

Note: Take the Mother Reserve out of the refrigerator the night before. Put 2 cups water in a large bowl, glass or stainless steel, add the Mother Reserve and 2 cups of flour and 1 tablespoon sugar. Mix well. Cover and let set overnight. Next morning take out your Mother Reserve and return it to the refrigerator for future use. Use what is left in bowl for your bread.

Strawberry Sourdough Bread

1½ cups all-purpose
Gold Medal Flour
½ teaspoon baking soda
¾ cup sugar
2 eggs
1½ cups sliced strawberries
1 cup chopped walnuts
¾ cup sourdough starter

In a large bowl lightly beat the eggs. Mix in the oil and sugar, and sourdough. Add the flour and soda. Stir until flour is just blended. Fold in the strawberries and walnuts. Do not overblend or the bread may be tough. Butter and lightly flour an 8½x4½-inch loaf pan. Pour the batter into pan and bake on center rack in oven for 1 hour and 20 minutes at 350°, or until an inserted toothpick comes out clean.

Turn out on wire rack to cool. Cut into squares and serve.

This is very good with a Sunday Morning Brunch served warm with fresh strawberry jam.

Also very good served with strawberries and whipped cream.

Bread Stuffing Made With Sourdough Bread

Bread stuffing is popular for roast poultry. For making it, bread that is at least a day old is better than fresh. Take your day old bread and cut or break it into strips ½ by 1-inch pieces. Let the pieces dry for another day.

This recipe can be doubled, depending on the size of the turkey.

This recipe is for a 14 pound turkey.

2 quarts bread crumbs
⅔ cup fat (Butter)
1 cup finely chopped celery
1 cup finely chopped onion
¾ teaspoon salt
2 teaspoons ground sage (more or less depending on your taste)
3 eggs
1 can cream of mushroom soup
1 small clove of garlic, mashed
¼ teaspoon coarse ground pepper
enough chicken broth to make the dressing moist

Melt fat in a skillet, add the celery, garlic and onion. Cook until the onion is clear. Add all other ingredients together. Add onion mixture and mix well. Stuff the washed and patted dry turkey.

OYSTER STUFFING: Add ½ pint of oysters heated in 1 tablespoon of butter. Drain, chop and add to stuffing.

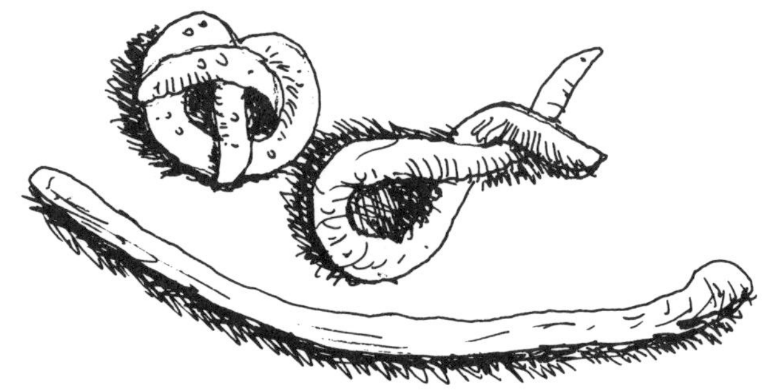

Sourdough Whole Wheat Pretzel

Set starter the night before with your reserve starter. Add 1½ cups water, 1½ cups flour (white), your reserve starter and 1 tablespoon sugar. Mix thoroughly, cover and let set overnight. The next morning take out your reserve and return it to the refrigerator. (Always use glass or stainless steel to mix up your starter in.)

Pretzel:

1½ cups all-purpose flour
1½ cups milk
¼ cup honey
1 teaspoon salt
2 cups whole wheat flour

1 egg white
1 tablespoon water
2 tablespoons poppy seed, sesame
    seed or grated cheese (Parmesan)
Mustard (optional)

In the starter sponge that is left in the bowl you are now ready to mix your pretzels.

Heat the milk, honey and salt till lukewarm. Add to the starter. Mix well, (about 1 minute), scraping bowl. BEAT at high speed with electric mixer for another 3 minutes. Add the whole wheat flour. Using a wooden spoon, mix well. If more flour is needed add the white flour in small amounts at a time. Turn onto a floured board. Knead in enough flour to make a moderately stiff dough 8 to 10 minutes. Shape into a ball. Place into a greased bowl, turning once to grease both sides. Cover and let rise until double in size, about 1 hour. Punch down. Turn out onto a lightly floured surface. Cover and let rest for 10 minutes. Divide dough into 4 portions. Divide 1 portion into 9 small pieces (36 pieces total or more). Roll each piece into a rope about 12 inches long. Shape rope into a circle, overlapping about 4 inches from each end; leave ends free. Take one end of dough in each hand and twist at the point where dough overlaps (see photo).

Carefully lift ends across to opposite edges of the circle. Tuck ends under edge for pretzel shape; moisten and press to seal. Repeat with rest of dough. Let rise, uncovered for at least 20 minutes. Meanwhile in a 3 quart Dutch oven bring 2 quarts water and 2 tablespoons of salt to boiling. Lower four or five pretzels at a time into the boiling water; boil for 2 minutes turning once. Remove from water with a slotted spoon. Drain a few seconds on a wire rack. Place ½ inch apart on a well-greased baking sheet. Brush with egg white mixed with water. Sprinkle with poppy seed, sesame seed or Parmesan cheese. Bake in a 350° F. oven for 25 to 30 minutes or until golden brown. Repeat with all remaining dough. Serve with mustard.

Winter Squash Sourdough Bread

Lee Cole from Douglas, Wyoming wanted a recipe to make squash sourdough bread. She gave me some ingredients from an old recipe that she had. Using some of the ingredients, I came up with this wonderful squash bread, made with Old Mother Hubbard Squash.

Set your starter the night before, by dipping out 1/2 cup of your Mother Reserve, (be sure to add back 1/4 cup water and 1/4 cup of flour to your Mother Reserve Pot). To the 1/2 cup of starter add 1 cup water, 1 cup flour and 1 tablespoon sugar. Cover and let set over night.

Cook enough squash to make 2 cups of mashed squash.

Bread
1 1/2 cups sourdough starter sponge
1 cup dark brown sugar
1 teaspoon ginger
1/2 teaspoon salt
1/4 teaspoon nutmeg
1/4 teaspoon cinnamon
2 cups winter squash
1/2 cup milk
1/2 cup butter melted
7 to 8 cups flour

Mix as directed: to the 1 1/2 cups of starter add the melted butter, add all the other ingredients in order. Kneed until smooth and elastic. About 3 to 5 minutes. Set in greased bowl and cover with a damp cloth. Let rise until double in size. Make into 3 small loaves or 2 larger ones. Let double in size. Bake in pre-heated 375°F. oven for 45 minutes or until done.

This is also very good with 1 1/2 cups raisins.

Sourdough Rye Bread

Set your sourdough starter sponge the night before you bake. Using 2 cups water, 2 cups flour, 1 tablespoon sugar, add your Mother Reserve and beat until smooth. Cover and let set overnight. Next morning take out your Mother Reserve and return to the refrigerator for future use. Be sure to sprinkle a dash of sugar on top and leave uncovered.

Now for the bread:

2 cups rye flour, unsifted
1 pkg. yeast, active dry
(may be omitted)
1 tablespoon sugar
2 teaspoons salt
1 tablespoon caraway seeds
2 tablespoons shortening
Enough white flour to make
dough easy to work

If you use yeast, mix as directed on package. Add to starter. Now mix in the sugar, salt and caraway seeds. Melt the shortening and add to the starter mixture. Now add the 2 cups of rye flour and mix thoroughly. Add more white flour if needed to make a nice smooth and workable dough. Knead on a lightly floured board until dough is smooth and elastic, for 10 minutes or 300 strokes.

Place into a greased bowl, turn over to get grease on both sides. Cover with a wet cloth and let rise until double in size. Press down to remove air bubbles. Divide dough in half, round each half to a ball, cover and let rest for 10 minutes. Now shape into desired shape, either round or into a loaf 8 inches long. Place on greased baking sheet. Cover and let rise until double in size. Bake in a preheated oven 375° F. for 50 minutes.

Sourdough Honey Whole Wheat Gingerbread

¾ cup honey
¾ cup oil
1 cup molasses
3 eggs
½ cup sourdough starter
1 teaspoon salt
3 cups sifted whole wheat flour
1½ teaspoons cloves
3 teaspoons baking powder
1 teaspoon ginger
1½ teaspoons cinnamon
2 cups milk

Mix honey, oil, molasses and eggs together. Mix in sourdough starter. Set aside. Sift together all the dry ingredients. Add this flour mixture to the honey mixture, alternately with the milk. Pour into a greased 9x13-inch pan. Bake at 325° oven for 40 minutes or until done.

Sourdough Whole Wheat Potato Bread

Set oven 375° F.

Set starter sponge the night before by putting 1½ cups water, 1½ cups flour (white), 1 tablespoon sugar, and Mother Reserve. Mix well, cover and let set overnight. Next morning take out Mother Reserve and return to refrigerator.

Ingredients for bread:

1½ cups starter sponge
1 cup milk
1 cup mashed potatoes
(instant may be used)
1 teaspoon salt
1 tablespoon caraway seeds
(can be omitted)
4 cups whole wheat flour
4 tablespoons cornmeal

In a large mixing bowl combine milk with sourdough starter, mashed potatoes, salt and caraway seeds; mix well. Stir in flour and mix until stiff. Turn out onto a floured board and mix until a smooth and elastic dough forms. Work for 10 minutes. Turn into a greased bowl and cover. Let rise until double in size. Punch down and make into 2 round loaves. Grease two 8-inch pans. Dust with the cornmeal. Place bread into pans. Cover and let rise again until double in size. Brush loaves with water and split top with a sharp knife in a criss-cross fashion. Bake 375° F. for 50 minutes.

Sourdough Whole Wheat Bread

4 cups starter
3 tablespoons melted butter
1½ teaspoons salt
4½ cups whole wheat flour

Take Mother Reserve from refrigerator the night before. Put 2 cups tepid water in large bowl or stainaless steel pan, add Mother Reserve, 1 tablespoon sugar and 2 cups of white flour. Beat until thick or like sponge. Cover and let set overnight. Next morning take out Mother Reserve, sprinkle a little sugar over top and set back into refrigerator for future use.

In remaining 4 cups of sponge add 1½ teaspoons salt, 3 tablespoons melted butter, and 4 cups of whole wheat flour. Work until easy to handle, adding more flour if needed.

Turn out on floured board where ½ cup of the whole wheat flour has been added. Leaven 300 strokes or until smooth and spongy. Put into greased bowl, let rise until double in size. Punch down and put into two loaf pans which have been greased. Let rise again until double in size. Bake in 375° oven for 50 minutes.

Biscuit Mix

8 cups sifted Gold Medal flour
4 teaspoons salt
¼ cup baking powder
Sift all together
Cut into mix 1 cup
lard or butter

Mix well. Store in large jar in refrigerator.

For one recipe of biscuits use ½ cup milk, ½ cup sourdough starter to 2 cups mix. Depending on the consistency of your starter more milk may be needed. The dough should be easy to manage and not too stiff. Bake at 425° F. for 12 to 15 minutes.

Another biscuit mix that I use that has less salt, less fat and is very, very good is:

8 cups flour
3 teaspoons salt
4 tablespoons baking powder
6 oz. butter

Blend all ingredients together in blender until butter is the size of small peas.

Biscuit mix should be kept in the refrigerator or may be frozen.

For one recipe of biscuits use 2 cups of mix, add ½ cup sourdough starter and ½ cup milk. More milk may be added if needed.

Sourdough Buttermilk Biscuits

2 cups unsifted all-purpose flour
½ tablespoon baking soda
2 teaspoons baking powder
½ teaspoon salt
2 tablespoons butter, melted
⅔ cup buttermilk
1 cup sourdough starter

Preheat oven to 450° F.

Combine flour, baking soda, salt and baking powder into a large bowl. Add buttermilk, melted butter and sourdough starter. Stir well. Turn onto a floured board and knead lightly. Pat dough until ⅔ inch thick. Cut with a 2½ inch round cutter.

Place biscuits on greased baking sheet. Brush top with melted butter and bake 12 to 15 minutes. Serve hot with honey butter.

Be sure that you set your starter the night before you bake. Take your Mother Reserve out of the refrigerator and mix with ½ cup water, ½ cup flour and a dash of sugar. Cover and let set until the next morning. Put Mother Reserve back into refrigerator. Use 1 cup of leftover starter for your biscuits. If you dip a cup of starter out of your Mother Reserve be sure to add the same amount of water and flour back to the reserve.

Buttermilk Sourdough Chive Biscuits

6 cups all-purpose flour
1 teaspoon salt
¼ cup baking powder
2 tablespoons sugar
¼ cup chopped chives, fresh
1 cup butter
3 cups sourdough starter sponge
1½ cups buttermilk

Preheat oven to 400°.

Mix flour, baking powder, salt, and sugar in a large bowl. Stir in chives. Cut in butter until mixture resembles coarse crumbs. Stir in buttermilk and starter. Knead lightly on floured board. Cut into biscuits and put onto greased cookie sheet. Bake 12 to 15 minutes. Makes 36 biscuits.

Sourdough Cheddar Cheese Biscuits

Set oven to 425°

2 cups all-purpose Gold
Medal Flour, unsifted
1 tablespoon baking powder
¼ teaspoon salt
2 tablespoons melted butter
½ cup sourdough starter
1 cup whole milk (or ½ cup condensed
milk mixed with ½ cup water)
1 cup shredded sharp cheddar cheese

Mix flour, baking powder and salt. Mix milk and melted butter together. Add to flour mixture along with starter. Add shredded cheese. Stir just until the flour is dampened. Turn onto floured board and pat down lightly. Cut into 12 biscuits. Put onto a greased baking sheet. Bake at 425° for 12 to 15 minutes.

Sourdough Sour Cream-Onion Biscuits

2 cups unsifted all-purpose flour
1 tablespoon baking powder
1½ teaspoon onion powder
1 teaspoon sugar
1 teaspoon salt
½ cup butter
½ cup sourdough starter
1 cup dairy sour cream

Into a medium bowl, measure flour, baking powder, onion powder, sugar and salt. Cut in butter and mix until mixture resembles coarse crumbs.

Add sour cream and sourdough starter, stirring until mixture is moistened. Turn dough onto lightly floured surface. Knead about 10 times to form a soft smooth dough.

Gently roll or pat to ¾ inch thickness. Cut with a 2½ inch cutter. Place on ungreased cookie sheet. Bake until golden brown. About 12 minutes in 425° F. oven or 10 minutes in 450° oven.

Four of us left the ranch at daylight on horseback to gather cows and calves from the north slopes of the Ferris mountains. By mid-afternoon the gather had been thrown onto the flats and we headed for a sheepherders camp in hope of finding food. The sheepwagon was deserted. The door opened to the clear, clean mountain air with the traditional crock of sourdough quietly working near the stove. Dismounting, we gathered a handful of rocks and proceeded to obtain our dinner from a covey of fool hens feeding near the wagon. A fire was set in the stove to fry up a skillet of fool hens, boil potatoes and bake a pan of sourdough rolls rising in the heat. The memory of that excellent meal and the odors of frying fool hens and sourdough bread baking in the hot wood stove will remain with me forever.

Robbie Duncan

Sourdough Biscuits

2 cups flour
3 tablespoons butter or shortening
½ cup sourdough starter
½ teaspoon salt
1 tablespoon baking powder
1 cup milk or buttermilk
(if buttermilk is used cut butter back to 2 tablespoons)

Sift flour, baking power and salt into bowl; cut in butter or shortening until mixture resembles coarse crumbs. Add milk and sourdough and mix until dough moves around easily in bowl.

Turn out onto floured surface. Knead gently, pat ½ inch thick and cut with biscuit cutter.

Bake on lightly greased cookie sheet in very hot oven (450°) 12 to 15 minutes.

True Sourdough Biscuits

2 cups sourdough starter
1½ cups Gold Medal Flour
½ teaspoon salt
2 tablespoons melted butter
(shortening or bacon grease
may be used)

Mix all ingredients together until dough is soft but manageable. Put onto lightly floured board and knead lightly. Cut and let rise until double in size, about 40 minutes. Bake in a preheated oven 425° for 20 minutes.

Note: Be sure to set your starter the night before; 2 cups water, 2 cups flour and your Mother Reserve. Mix well, cover and let set overnight. Put your reserve back into the refrigerator.

Sourdough Whole Wheat Biscuits

1 cup sourdough starter
1 cup all-purpose white flour
1 cup whole wheat flour
1 tablespoon baking powder
1 teaspoon salt
⅓ cup butter or shortening
¾ cup milk, more if needed

Mix dry ingredients thoroughly. Mix in butter with a pastry blender or two knives until the mixture is crumbly. Stir in the milk and sourdough. Add more milk if dough is too stiff. Dough should be soft and easy to roll out but not sticky.

Knead on a floured board a few times. Pat or roll dough to 1 inch thick. Cut with a biscuit cutter or squares with a knife. Place biscuits on a greased baking sheet close together for soft sides or 1 inch apart for crusty sides.

Bake 12 to 15 minutes until golden brown. Calories per biscuit about 135.

Sourdough Old Fashioned Cinnamon Buns

½ cup sugar
½ teaspoon salt
2 cups Sourdough starter (see note)
1 cup milk
¼ cup butter
1 egg
about 4 cups all-purpose
  Gold Medal flour
½ cup firmly packed brown sugar
½ cup white sugar
½ cup finely chopped walnuts
½ cup raisins
2½ teaspoons cinnamon
⅔ cup softened butter

Sugar glaze – 1 cup confectioners sugar plus 4 teaspoons melted butter, and enough real dairy cream to make a smooth paste. You may add rum or vanilla.

In a bowl combine sugar, salt and sourdough starter. In a saucepan heat milk and ¼ cup butter until warm. Add milk and butter mixture to starter. Now add the one egg and beat well. Stir in the rest of the flour one cup at a time. Turn out onto a floured board and knead until smooth. Add more flour if needed, a little at a time. Put into a well greased bowl and let rise until double in size. Punch down and roll out into a square. Combine the sugars. Spread the softened butter onto the dough. Sprinkle the sugars evenly. Now dust with the cinnamon, raisins and walnuts. Roll and cut into 1 inch pieces. Put cut side down in a greased pan. Let rise again until double in size. Cook in a 375° oven for 30 minutes. Frost while still warm.

Note: Take your Mother Reserve out of refrigerator the night before and add 2 cups of water, 2 cups of gold medal flour, your Mother Reserve and 1 tablespoon sugar. Let set overnight. Next morning return your Mother Reserve to refrigerator.

Sourdough Sticky Buns

2 cups Sourdough starter, see note
1 cup lukewarm milk
¼ cup sugar
¼ pound butter
4 cups all-purpose flour,
mixed with 1 teaspoon salt
2 egg yolks
2 tablespoons cinnamon, mixed
with ¼ cup white sugar
½ cup raisins or currants
½ cup water, mixed with 2 cups
firmly packed brown sugar
4 tablespoons butter
1 cup walnuts left in halves

Put the milk into a pan and heat until tiny bubbles form. Add the 4 tablespoons butter and ¼ cup sugar and heat until butter is melted. Cool. Add to the starter. Beat egg yolks and add to the starter. Now work 3½ cups flour into the sponge and work until dough becomes firm. Turn out onto board floured with the last ½ cup flour and knead 300 strokes. More flour may be sprinkled on board if needed. Shape the dough into a ball and put into a buttered bowl. Cover with a damp cloth and let rise until double in size. In a small heavy pan combine the ½ cup water, brown sugar and 4 tablespoons butter. Stir until all the sugar dissolves bringing to a boil over high heat. Reduce heat to moderate and cook until syrup has a color of maple syrup. Let the syrup cool slightly, then dribble half of it into a buttered 8x8-inch pan. Add the walnut halves. While syrup is cooling punch the dough down and transfer it to a floured board and roll into a rectangle 14 inches long and ¼ to ½ inch thick. Brush the dough with 4 tablespoons of melted butter. Sprinkle with the cinnamon and sugar mixture. Sprinkle the raisins on top. Now pour the rest of the remaining half of the syrup over the top of the raisins. Roll into a cylinder about 2 inches in diameter. Cut into 1 inch rounds and place cut side down into the syrup. Cover and let rise until double in size.

Bake in a preheated oven 350° for 40 minutes or until done. Remove to a rack placed over a platter and cool.

Note: Take your Mother Reserve out of refrigerator the night before and add 2 cups of water, 2 cups of gold medal flour, your Mother Reserve and 1 tablespoon sugar. Let set overnight. Next morning take Mother Reserve back out and save for future use. Use remaining sponge for buns.

Sourdough Cakes And Cookies
And Other Recipes

Sourdough Fresh Ground Applesauce Cake

½ cup sourdough
½ cup sugar
1 egg
½ cup butter (or shortening)
1½ cups fresh chopped
 or ground apples
1 cup raisins
2 cups all-purpose Gold Medal Flour
½ teaspoon salt
1 teaspoon soda
1 teaspoon cinnamon
½ teaspoon cloves
½ teaspoon allspice

Cream butter, sugar and egg. Add sourdough starter. Add fresh ground apples and raisins. Stir in all other ingredients. Pour into a greased and floured pan 9x13x2-inch. Bake 350° F. for 30 to 40 minutes. Frost with favorite frosting.

Sourdough Buttermilk Cake

1 cup sugar
½ cup shortening
1 teaspoon nutmeg
1 teaspoon cinnamon
½ teaspoon cloves
pinch of salt
½ cup sourdough starter
1 cup raisins
1 teaspoon soda
1 cup buttermilk
2 eggs
2½ cups all-purpose
 Gold Medal flour

Mix spices, salt and sugar. Cream shortening and add sugar and spices. Sift soda with flour. Add sourdough starter. Add buttermilk and raisins. Beat eggs, add to mixture and beat well. Add flour and soda to mixture and beat well. Pour into a greased and floured loaf pan. Bake in a 350° F. oven for 50 minutes or until done.

Sourdough has been around for centuries. The first time that I was aware of it was when I was a young girl. My grandmother Larive had a crock of sourdough behind the old wood cook stove in the kitchen. I was not much into sourdough when I was young and really not into it when I got a "whiff" of it when Grandma lifted the loose lid and scraped the "green stuff" off the top and tossed it away. Then she proceeded to scoop out a bowl full of the starter and took it to the old kitchen cupboard where she now mixed up a batch of pancakes for breakfast. I remember my uncles eating them like there would be no more. They were getting ready to go thrash grain that day (gosh, how I loved hearing those old thrashing machines run). I finally decided to try one and was surprised at the wonderful taste. One that I remembered for a long, long time.

Grandmother Larive later put a couple cups of flour and a couple of more cups of water into the crock, stirred it up and replaced the lid. Sourdough pancakes are a must in our house today. Add a few huckleberries or blueberries and they really become a treat.

Carrot Cake

1½ cups sugar
3 eggs
½ cup oil
1½ cups flour
1 teaspoon baking powder
1 teaspoon soda
½ cup sourdough
½ teaspoon salt
1 teaspoon cinnamon
½ teaspoon nutmeg
1 teaspoon vanilla
¼ cup rum
1 cup nuts
½ cup raisins
1½ cups ground carrots

Grind carrots, raisins and nuts in grinder; set aside. Mix sugar, oil and eggs together. Add all other ingredients together. Mix well.

Bake in round bundt pan for 50 minutes at 325°.

This is very good with a rum frosting.

Brandy or Rum Butter Frosting

Cream ¼ pound butter, 1 pound powdered sugar, 3 tablespoons or ⅓ cup rum or brandy and table cream to bring a smooth, creamy frosting. This frosting adds a great deal to an applesauce cake or carrot cake. Add more or less rum or brandy and smooth out with cream, a teaspoon at a time.

Sourdough Chiffon Cake

1⅓ cups all-purpose flour
¾ cup sugar
1½ teaspoons double-acting
  baking powder
½ teaspoon salt
¼ cup crisco oil
¼ cup water, cold
4 egg yolks
½ cup sourdough starter
½ teaspoon vanilla
1 tablespoon fresh lemon juice
¼ teaspoon cream of tarter
4 egg whites

Mix and sift the first four ingredients. Make a well and add the crisco oil, water, egg yolks, sourdough starter, vanilla and lemon juice. Beat until smooth. Now add the cream of tarter to the egg whites. Beat the whites until they form very stiff peaks. Gently fold the flour mixture into the egg whites until well blended. Be sure to fold very gently. Turn into an ungreased 9-inch tube pan. Bake for 1 hour in moderate overn 325° F. Cake should spring back when touched with finger. Immediately turn pan upside down placing tube over neck of bottle. Let hang to cool. Loosen with spatula to remove from pan.

Frost with a berry frosting:
2 cups powdered sugar, ⅛ teaspoon salt, 4 tablespoons butter (softened) and 1 cup strawberries blended in a blender. Mix all ingredients together until smooth. Spread over top of cooled cake.

Sourdough Chocolate Cake

1 cup starter
1 cup milk
1 cup sugar
½ cup shortening
½ teaspoon salt
1½ teaspoon baking soda
1 teaspoon vanilla
1 teaspoon cinnamon
2 eggs
3 squares semi-sweet
 chocolate, melted
2 cups flour

Prepare starter the night before (see below). Cream sugar and shortening together, add eggs and mix until smooth. Add sourdough starter, milk, vanilla, cinnamon and melted chocolate. Beat at least 2 minutes. Blend salt and soda into the flour and add to mixture; fold in gently but thoroughly. Pour into greased and floured cake pans. Bake at 350° for 35 to 40 minutes.

To prepare starter, take Mother Reserve from refrigerator and add 1 cup water, 1 cup starter, and 1 teaspoon sugar. Mix thoroughly. Cover and let set overnight. Next morning put Mother Reserve starter back into refrigerator for future use.

Sour Cream Sourdough Chocolate Cake

3 squares chocolate
½ cup water
1 cube butter
1½ cups sugar
½ cup sourdough
2 cups cake flour
1 teaspoon soda
¼ teaspoon salt
3 eggs
1 cup or more sour cream
1 teaspoon vanilla

Melt chocolate in water over low heat. Cool. Cream butter, sugar and add sourdough starter. Add eggs and sour cream. Stir lightly. Add flour, soda and salt and beat for 2 minutes. Add chocolate and vanilla. Mix well. Grease and flour 2 8x8-inch pans. Pour half of dough into each pan and bake at 375° for 30 to 35 minutes. Cool and frost with cocoa and powdered sugar icing.

Powdered Sugar Cocoa Frosting

2 cups powdered sugar, sifted with 3 tablespoons cocoa
4 tablespoons melted butter
1 teaspoon vanilla
3 tablespoons canned milk or cream
Beat until smooth

Sourdough Fruit Cocktail Cake

This was always a favorite of the crew when I was working at a Ranch in Idaho's primitive area.

2 cups flour
1½ cups sugar
1 teaspoon soda
½ cup sourdough starter
1 teaspoon salt
1 medium sized can fruit cocktail

Mix and beat well. Pour into a greased and floured 8x13-inch pan. Sprinkle top of cake with ½ cup brown sugar and ½ cup of nut meats.

Bake in 350° F. oven for 45 minutes or until done.

Dressing For Top

1 cup canned milk
1 stick margerine or butter
¾ cup sugar

Boil for 4 minutes. Add 1 teaspoon vanilla. Spread over the cake then sprinkle the top with coconut.

Sourdough Golden Fig Cake

This fig cake is wonderful for the holiday season. May be baked in a bundt pan or tube pan. Serve with a brandy hard sauce.

2½ cups flour
1 teaspoon salt
1 teaspoon soda
1 teaspoon nutmeg
½ teaspoon cinnamon
¼ teaspoon cloves
1 cup chopped walnuts
1½ cups dried figs
1¼ cups chopped dates
1¼ cups mixed diced
candied fruits and peels
1 cup raisins
¾ cup candied cherries
1 cup butter
1 cup sugar
5 eggs
1 cup sourdough starter
¼ cup light corn syrup
¼ cup brandy
Hard Sauce

Sift together 1½ cups flour with salt, soda and spices. Mix remaining 1 cup flour with the walnuts, figs, dates, fruits and peels, raisins and cherries, separating pieces. Cream the butter and sugar until light and fluffy. Add eggs one at a time, beating thoroughly after each addition. Add corn syrup, sourdough starter and brandy. Add the flour mixture, stirring to blend. Add the fruit and nut mixture, stirring to blend well. Turn into a well greased 10-inch tube pan or Bundt pan. Set another pan containing 2 cups water on bottom shelf of oven. Place cake on middle shelf and bake at 300° F. for 2¼ hours or until knife inserted comes out clean. Cool cake in pan for 30 minutes. Turn out on wire rack to finish cooling. Wrap in foil and let stand at room temperature overnight. May be stored in refrigerator for several weeks. Serve with brandied hard sauce.

Brandied Hard Sauce

⅔ cup butter - softened
¼ teaspoon nutmeg
2 cups sifted powdered sugar
2 tablespoons brandy or rum

Combine butter and nutmeg. Blend well. Add sugar alternately with brandy or rum and blend well. Makes 1½ cups. Put into dish and serve with Christmas Pudding.

This may be made up a couple of days ahead and kept in the refrigerator. Keeps up to three weeks.

Sourdough Quaker Fruit Cake

1½ cups brown sugar
2 eggs
1 cup sour milk
½ cup shortening
½ cup sourdough starter
2 cups flour plus 2 tablespoons
1 teaspoon soda
1 teaspoon nutmeg
½ teaspoon allspice
1 cup chopped walnuts
1 package fruit mix (candied)
1 cup raisins
1 teaspoon vanilla
1 cup chopped dates

Mix sugar with eggs, shortening, milk and sourdough starter. Add flour, spices, salt and baking soda. Mix well. Add remaining ingredients and mix well. Pour into floured and greased pan. Bake in 300° F. oven for 1½ hours. Place a cup of hot water in oven with cake while baking.

Sourdough Ice Cream Cake

1 cube butter
1½ cups sugar
1¾ cups all-purpose
Gold Medal flour
5 egg whites
2 teaspoons baking powder
2 teaspoons vanilla
½ cup sourdough starter sponge
1 cup cold water

Cream together butter, sugar and vanilla. Beat egg whites until very stiff. Mix sourdough starter with 1 cup of cold water. Add the flour to the butter mixture along with the water and sourdough. Add the beaten egg whites and gently fold into the flour mixture. Fold in the 2 teaspoons baking powder at last. Pour into greased and floured 8x8-inch pan. Bake in 350° oven for 30 to 35 minutes.

Sourdough Mayonnaise Cake

1 cup chopped dates
1 cup boiling water
1 teaspoon baking soda

Mix the above and set aside to cool.

1 cup mayonnaise
(I use Best Foods)
1 cup sugar
1 teaspoon vanilla
½ cup sourdough starter
¼ teaspoon salt
1 teaspoon cinnamon
½ teaspoon each nutmeg and cloves
2 cups all-purpose flour
dab of cream
1 cup chopped nuts
3 tablespoons cocoa
¼ cup cream

Mix mayonnaise and sugar. Sift flour, salt, cinnamon, nutmeg, cloves and cocoa together. Stir sourdough starter into mayonnaise mixture. Add dry ingredients alternately with water mixture and small amounts of cream. Add vanilla and nuts. Mix well. Turn into a well greased and floured tube pan (9-inch) and bake in a preheated oven 325° F. for 1 hour or until done.

Tasty Sourdough Pound Cake

2 cups flour
2 cups sugar
1 cup sourdough
1 teaspoon baking soda
¼ teaspoon salt
⅔ cup oil
6 eggs
1 teaspoon vanilla
1 square chocolate, melted
1½ teaspoons almond extract

Put all ingredients except the melted chocolate in a bowl and beat for 10 minutes. Put all but a small amount into a burnt pan, which has been greased and floured. Mix chocolate into the small remaining amount. Now swirl this chocolate mixed batter into the batter already in the burnt pan.

Bake at 350° for 1 hour. Drizzle with Chocolate Glaze.

Glossy Chocolate Glaze

Melt together on warm burner 3 tablespoons butter and 3 squares unsweetened chocolate.

Pour 5 tablespoons scalding hot milk over 2 cups sifted confectioner's sugar and ¼ teaspoon salt. Stir to dissolve completely.

Add 1 teaspoon vanilla and the chocolate mixture. It will be very thin. Beat while hot until it thickens enough to spread and becomes glossy. Add ½ cup chopped nuts if desired.

Sourdough Strawberry-Rhubarb Sponge Cake

Sponge-cake layers
6 eggs
1⅓ cups unsifted cake flour
½ cup sourdough starter sponge
1 teaspoon baking powder
¼ teaspoon salt
1 cup granulated sugar
⅓ cup cold water
1½ teaspoons vanilla
½ teaspoon cream of tarter

Strawberry-Rhubarb Filling
2 cups fresh or frozen rhubarb
cut into 1-inch pieces
2 tablespoons water
2 teaspoons cornstarch
3 tablespoons sugar
2 egg yolks
1 cup sliced strawberries (fresh)

Fluffy Frosting
2 egg whites
1⅓ cups granulated sugar
¼ cup cold water
¼ teaspoon cream of tarter
⅛ teaspoon salt
1½ teaspoons vanilla
Fresh strawberries

For the sponge cake, separate the eggs. Place the whites in a large bowl and the yolks in a medium sized bowl. Heat oven to 350° F. Grease and flour bottoms but not sides of three 8-inch cake pans. Sift flour, baking powder and salt together onto waxed paper. With electric beater, beat yolks until thick and lemon colored. Gradually beat in half of the sugar until very thick. Add sourdough starter, flour mixture, water and vanilla. Stir until smooth. Wash beaters. Add cream of tarter to the egg whites. Beat at high speed adding remaining sugar, one tablespoon at a time, until stiff peaks form when beaters are raised.

Gently fold egg-yolk mixture into the whites until uniformly mixed. Divide into pans. Bake 25 minutes. Remove pans to cool. Cool in pans 10 minutes. Loosen sides with a small spatula. Remove cakes to cooling racks. Cool completely.

Meanwhile, prepare filling:

In a heavy saucepan, bring rhubarb and 1 tablespoon water to a boil, covered over low heat. Continue to simmer gently, stirring occasionally until rhubarb is very tender. In a small bowl, stir together cornstarch and sugar. Add remaining water and stir until smooth. Stir the cornstarch mixture into the rhubarb mixture and cook until thickened. In the same bowl beat the egg yolks. Fold a little of the thickened rhubarb into the yolks. Return the yolks to the rhubarb and cook over low heat until mixture comes to a boil, stirring constantly. Remove from heat and fold in the strawberries. Set aside to cool.

When cake layers and filling are cool, assemble cake. Place one cake layer right-side up on serving plate. Top with half of filling. Place second layer on top of filling and put remaining half of filling on top. Put last layer on top. Refrigerate several hours. An hour before serving, make the frosting. Combine egg whites, sugar, cold water, cream of tarter, and salt in the top of a double boiler. Beat 1 minute. Place frosting over boiling water in double boiler. Beat with electric beater until frosting forms soft peaks when beater is lifted, about seven minutes. Remove pan from heat. Beat in vanilla, and continue to beat until frosting holds stiff peaks. Frost cake immediately. Decorate with fresh strawberries. Serve.

Sourdough Strawberry Shortcake

2 cups sourdough starter (see note)
1½ cups all-purpose
Gold Medal flour
6 tablespoons sugar
5 teaspoons baking powder
1 teaspoon salt
1½ quarter pounds butter,
chilled and cut into bits
1½ cups heavy cream
3 pints fresh strawberries
2 tablespoons sugar
2 pints heavy whipping cream

Preheat oven to 450°. Put flour, 6 tablespoons sugar, baking powder and salt into large bowl. Add butter and with fingers work the butter until it resembles a fine course meal. Pour in the 1½ cups cream and the starter. Mix until firm. Turn out onto a floured board and work slightly. Roll to 1 inch thick and cut with a 3 to 4-inch cookie cutter or use a large glass. Put on slightly buttered cookie sheet and bake in center of oven for 12 to 15 minutes. Check often to see if done.

Meanwhile chop one half of the strawberries and mix with 2 tablespoons sugar. Whip cream. Serve with sliced berries in the center of sliced shortcakes, topped with whipped cream and fresh berries.

Note: Mix your sponge the night before. Take your Mother Reserve from refrigerator and mix with 2 cups water, 2 cups flour and 1 tablespoon sugar. Cover and let set overnight. Next morning take your Mother Reserve back out and return to the refrigerator.

Grandma's Sourdough Sunday Cake

1 cup quick cook oatmeal
1¼ cups boiling water
1 stick butter
1 cup brown sugar
1 cup white sugar
2 eggs
½ cup sourdough starter
1½ cups flour
½ teaspoon soda
½ teaspoon nutmeg
1 teaspoon allspice
6 tablespoons butter
½ cup white sugar
1 cup coconut
½ cup canned milk
½ teaspoon vanilla
½ cup chopped pecans

Add oatmeal to boiling water, add butter. Cook 2 minutes stirring to prevent sticking. Set aside to cool. Mix sugar, eggs, flour, starter, soda, salt and spices. Then pour all together and mix well. Pour into a greased and floured 9x13 pan. Bake 40 minutes at 370° F. While cake is baking, mix together 6 tablespoons butter, ½ cup sugar, 1 cup coconut, ½ cup canned milk, ½ teaspoon vanilla and ½ cup pecans. Place mixture in refrigerator until cake is done. When cake is done, remove to cookie sheet. Spread frosting mixture evenly over cake and place under broiler until top begins to brown. Serve to Sunday company.

Sourdough Fresh Fruit Cobbler

⅔ to 1 cup sugar
1 tablespoon cornstarch
1 cup water
3 to 4 cups fresh fruit,
with juice
1 cup Gold Medal flour
3 tablespoons butter
½ cup sourdough starter
1 tablespoon sugar
1½ teaspoons baking powder
½ teaspoon salt
½ cup milk

Heat oven to 400° F.

Mix sugar, cornstarch and gradually stir in water. Bring to a boil for 1 minute stirring constantly. Fold in 1 cup of fruit. Slowly fold in the remaining fruit. Pour into a 1½ quart or 8x8-inch baking dish. Dot with butter. Sprinkle with cinnamon.

Measure 1 cup flour by dip method. Stir in sugar, baking powder and salt. Cut in butter until mixture looks like meal. Stir in milk and sourdough starter. Add a dash of cinnamon. Pour over or drop by spoonfuls over hot fruit. Bake 25 to 30 minutes. Serve warm with fresh cream or whipped cream.

Sourdough Chocolate Chip Cookies

4½ cups flour all-purpose
kind, unsifted
2 teaspoons soda
1 teaspoon salt
1 cup butter, softened
1 cup crisco, softened
1½ cups sugar
1¼ cups brown sugar, packed
2 teaspoons vanilla
1 cup sourdough starter
4 eggs
1¾ cup walnuts, chopped
2 12-ounce packages
chocolate chips

Preheat oven to 375°.

In a large bowl, combine butter, crisco, sugars and mix well. Add eggs and beat until all is blended. Add vanilla and sourdough starter. Beat in flour, soda, salt and mix well. Stir in walnuts and chocolate chips. Drop by tablespoons onto greased cookie sheet. Bake 10 to 12 minutes. This makes 70 cookies. Can be cut in half for smaller batches of cookies.

Sourdough Rolled Chocolate Cookies

2 cups all-purpose flour
½ cup sourdough starter
½ teaspoon salt
½ cup shortening, softened
¾ cup sugar
1 egg
2 tablespoons rum
1 teaspoon vanilla
2 ounces unsweetened chocolate, melted and cooled
1 cup uncooked quick oatmeal

Sift together the flour and salt into a bowl. Add the softened shortening, sugar, egg, rum, vanilla and sourdough starter. Add the melted chocolate. Beat until smooth. Add the oats, beat well. Chill for 1 hour in refrigerator. Roll on lightly floured board to ⅛ inch thick. Cut with cookie cutter. Place on ungreased cookie sheet. Bake in preheated oven 350° F. for 10 to 12 minutes.

Sourdough Oatmeal Chocolate Chip Cookies

½ cup butter
¾ cup brown sugar, packed
1 egg
1 teaspoon vanilla
1 cup flour, sifted
    pius 2 tablespoons
½ cup sourdough starter
½ teaspoon salt
½ teaspoon soda
1 6-ounce package semi-sweet
    chocolate chips or
    chocolate pieces
1 cup rolled oats

Cream together butter and sugar. Add egg, vanilla and sourdough starter and cream well. Add flour, salt and soda to the creamed mixture. Mix well. Add chocolate pieces and oats. Drop by teaspoons onto greased cookie sheet and bake at 375° F. oven 10 to 12 minutes.

Healthful Sourdough Oatmeal Cookies

½ cup butter
½ cup sourdough starter
½ cup vegetable shortening
1 cup brown sugar
1 cup white sugar
2 eggs
2 cups flour OR 1 cup each of white unbleached flour and whole wheat flour
1 teaspoon baking soda
1 teaspoon salt
1 teaspoon cinnamon
½ teaspoon nutmeg
2 cups oatmeal
⅛ cup wheat germ
1 cup raisins
1 cup grated carrots
½ cup pecans
1 teaspoon vanilla or rum extract

Cream butter, shortening and sugars. Add eggs one at a time, beating well after each. Add vanilla and sourdough starter. Mix all dry ingredients together, but do not sift. Add to the creamed mixture. Stir in the carrots, pecans and raisins. Drop by heaping teaspoons onto lightly greased cookie sheet. Bake at 375° for 12 to 15 minutes.

Sourdough Oatmeal Ginger Drops

2 cups all-purpose flour
1 teaspoon baking powder
½ teaspoon salt
¾ teaspoon cinnamon
¼ teaspoon baking soda
¾ teaspoon ginger
½ teaspoon cloves
½ cup soft shortening
½ cup firmly packed brown sugar
1 egg
½ cup light molasses
⅓ cup water
⅓ cup sourdough
1 cup rolled oats, uncooked

Mix and sift flour, baking powder, salt, baking soda and spices. Add shortening, sugar, sourdough starter, egg, molasses and water. Beat until smooth, about 2 minutes. Stir in oats. Drop onto cookie sheets, slightly greased. Bake at 375° for 10 to 12 minutes or until golden brown. Makes 3 dozen.

Kahlua Raisin Oatmeal Cookies

¼ cup butter – softened
¼ cup Best Foods Mayonnaise
½ cup crisco
2 eggs
¾ cup brown sugar
¾ cup granulated sugar
½ cup sourdough starter
½ cup Kahlua
2 tablespoons coffee
(saved from the morning pot)
1 cup raisins
1 teaspoon baking powder
1 teaspoon soda
½ teaspoon salt
2 cups all-purpose flour
2¾ cups old fashioned oatmeal
1 cup chopped walnuts

Put raisins into a small bowl and cover with the Kahlua and coffee. Let set for ½ hour. Cream butter, mayonnaise and crisco together. Add eggs. Mix well. Add sugars and mix until creamy. Add sourdough starter. Mix well. Add raisins and Kahlua, stir well. Mix flour, soda, salt and baking powder together. Add to bowl and mix. Add oatmeal and chopped nuts. Mix well. Drop by tablespoon onto greased cookie sheet. Bake in pre-heated oven 375° for 12 minutes.

Makes 32 cookies.

Sourdough Real Mayonnaise Oatmeal Cookies

1½ cups firmly packed dark brown sugar
¾ cup Best Foods mayonnaise
1 egg
2 teaspoons vanilla
3 cups old fashioned oats
½ cup sourdough starter
1 cup flour plus 2 tablespoons
1 teaspoon cinnamon
½ teaspoon soda
½ teaspoon nutmeg
¾ cup raisins

In a bowl mix the first four ingredients. Add the sourdough starter. Beat in oats, flour, cinnamon, nutmeg and soda. Add raisins. Drop by teaspoons three inches apart on greased cookie sheet. Bake 350° for 10 to 12 minutes or until brown. Transfer to wire rack to cool.

Sour Milk Sourdough Oatmeal Cookies

¾ cup shortening
1 cup sugar
2 eggs, beaten
2 cups all-purpose
Gold Medal flour
1 teaspoon baking powder
2 teaspoons cinnamon
1 teaspoon nutmeg
1 teaspoon cloves
1 teaspoon baking soda
1 cup raisins
2 cups old fashioned oatmeal
dash of salt
½ cup sour milk
½ cup sourdough starter

In a separate bowl, mix flour, baking powder, soda, salt, cinnamon, nutmeg and cloves. Set aside.

In large mixing bowl, mix shortening and sugar until smooth. Add eggs. Add sour milk and sourdough starter. Mix well. Add flour mixture and mix well. Add raisins and oatmeal. Mix until well blended. Add slightly more flour if needed. Drop onto a greased cookie sheet. Cook in a pre-heated oven 375° for 12 minutes or until done.

In the early forties, as a young girl, I used to ride with the United States Calvary. My parents were living on a farm near Sturgis, South Dakota, and the Calvary at Fort Mead used our back 40 acres to do Calvary maneuvers and target practice.

When they came riding by the ranch house Mother would see that they took along plenty of homemade cookies and hot bread for their lunch.

As the men dismounted, watered their horses and filled their canteens, my sister Rose and I would saddle our horses and beg to ride with them. We were not refused. We fell in behind the troops in double file and proudly rode to the drill pasture. We would have to stay in the tent with the Major when the men did their target practice drills. We played cards and helped set up the tables for lunch.

I remember how absolutely impressed I was looking up at the elegant polished black boots you could see your face in, the saddles that squeaked and blue, blue rifles in their scabbards. The horses that were so well groomed and the tails were tied. God, "to just ride one of those horses." How in the world did they ever find so many beautiful horses, all stamped on the rump with a US?

How proud we were when the Lieutenant would call, "Fall in line, ladies," and we would ride back home.

The bread and cookies were a great treat for the boys who were so far away from home. Mom said she often got many thank-you's from the Calvary for helping to keep up the morale.

The Calvary is gone from Fort Mead now. The grounds are now a V.A. Hospital. A museum is there to remind us that the calvary was there at one time. The old rock stables still stand. In revisiting Fort Mead it brought back the memories of days long ago.

Sourdough Raisin Date Oatmeal Cookies

(Tillie Larive)

½ cup sifted flour
½ teaspoon baking soda
½ teaspoon salt
½ cup firmly packed
  light brown sugar
⅓ cup butter or margerine
½ cup sourdough starter
1½ cups quick rolled oats
Raisin Date Filling
  See Note

Sift flour, baking soda, salt and stir in brown sugar. With a knife blend in butter. Stir in the sourdough and oats. Press half of the mixture in bottom of an 8x8x2-inch pan. Spread with raisin filling and cover with remaining mixture.

Note: Raisin Filling

1 cup raisins
1 cup chopped dates
½ cup granulated sugar
1 tablespoon grated
  orange rind
¼ cup orange juice

Mix all ingredients in a small saucepan, stirring occasionally while cooking on moderate heat until thickened. About 10 minutes. Cool.

Bake 350° for 30 minutes. Cool. Cut into squares. May frost with powdered sugar frosting.

Sourdough Oatmeal Cookies

1 cup raisins
1 cup water
¾ cup shortening
1½ cups sugar
2 eggs
½ cup sourdough starter
1 teaspoon vanilla
2½ cups Gold Medal flour
1 teaspoon soda
1 teaspoon salt
1 teaspoon cinnamon
½ teaspoon cloves
2 cups oatmeal
½ cup chopped nuts

Simmer raisins and water over medium heat until raisins are plump. About 15 minutes. Drain raisins, reserving the liquid. Add enough water to reserve liquid to measure ½ cup. Heat oven to 400°. Mix shortening, sugar, eggs, sourdough starter and vanilla. Stir in reserve liquid. Blend in the remaining ingredients. Bake on greased cookie sheet for 8 to 10 minutes.

Pecan Jumbles With Sourdough

1½ cups firmly
  packed dark brown sugar
1 cup Best Foods mayonnaise
2 eggs
1 teaspoon vanilla
¼ cup sourdough starter
2¾ cups unsifted flour
½ teaspoon soda
¼ teaspoon salt
1 cup chopped pecans
1 cup pecan halves

In a large bowl combine the first five ingredients. Beat until smooth. Stir in remaining ingredients. Drop by level tablespoon on greased cookie sheet. Top each cookie with a ½ pecan. Cook in oven at 375° F. for 8 to 10 minutes.

Sourdough Pumpkin Drop Cookies

1 cup sugar
1 egg
½ cup melted butter
1 teaspoon vanilla
½ cup sourdough starter
½ cup pumpkin, solid packed, either fresh or canned
2 cups all-purpose flour
¼ teaspoon salt
¼ teaspoon cloves
½ teaspoon nutmeg
½ teaspoon cinnamon
1 teaspoon soda
½ cup raisins
½ cup chopped nut meats

Mix sugar, egg, melted butter, vanilla and sourdough starter together in mixing bowl. Cream until smooth. Add the remaining ingredients and mix thoroughly. Drop by tablespoon onto a greased cookie sheet. Bake at 375° F. for 12 to 15 minutes.

Frost with a butter-powdered sugar frosting. Makes 26 cookies.

Butter Frosting
2 cups powdered sugar
5 tablespoons butter, melted
3 tablespoons rich cream, more if needed
1 teaspoon vanilla

Mix as given, spread on top of cookies when cool.

Honey Sourdough Pumpkin Drop Cookies

½ cup shortening
½ cup brown sugar, firmly packed
½ cup honey
2 eggs
1 cup cooked pumpkin
2 cups sifted flour
½ teaspoon baking powder
½ cup sourdough starter
½ teaspoon salt
½ teaspoon cinnamon
½ teaspoon cloves
½ teaspoon ginger
½ teaspoon nutmeg
1 cup chopped walnuts
1 cup raisins

Cream together shortening, brown sugar and honey. Add eggs and beat well. Add pumpkin with flour that has been sifted with baking powder and spices. Add sourdough starter and beat well. Drop by mounds onto a greased cookie sheet. Bake in moderate oven 375° for 15 to 18 minutes, or until done and lightly brown. Cool. May be frosted. Makes about 6 dozen small deliciously tender cookies.

Sourdough Pumpkin Cookies

½ cup sourdough starter
½ cup shortening
1¼ cups brown sugar
1½ cups cooked pumpkin
2 eggs, beaten
½ teaspoon salt
¼ teaspoon ginger
½ teaspoon nutmeg
½ teaspoon cinnamon
2½ cups all-purpose flour
2 teaspoons baking powder
1 cup raisins or currants
1 cup chopped pecans
1 teaspoon vanilla
 or lemon extract

Cream shortening and brown sugar thoroughly. Add eggs, pumpkin, and sourdough starter. Add seasonings. Blend well.

Sift flour and baking powder together. Stir in the raisins and pecans. Add the flour mixture to the creamed mixture and beat well. Blend in the vanilla or lemon extract.

Drop from teaspoons onto greased cookie sheet. Bake 15 minutes at 375° F. Makes 36 cookies.

Lunch Box Raisin Spice Squares

I carried these to school many times when I was a young girl. Sometimes they would freeze in the lunch box, walking to the bus. But would unthaw before lunch time. Not too many people carry lunches these days. However, very good for any meal.

2 cups all-purpose flour
1 teaspoon baking soda
1 teaspoon ground cinnamon
1 teaspoon ground nutmeg
½ teaspoon salt
1 cup raisins
1 cup water
½ cup rum (may omit rum but
  add ½ cup more water)
½ cup sourdough starter
1 egg
½ cup vegetable shortening
1 cup sugar
½ cup chopped walnuts
Orange Frosting
  (recipe follows)

Preheat oven to 350° F. Grease a 13x9x2-inch baking pan. Sift flour, baking soda, cinnamon, nutmeg and salt, set aside. Boil raisins rapidly in the 1½ cups water, or 1 cup water and ½ cup rum, in a medium saucepan for 10 minutes. Transfer raisins and liquid to a large bowl. Cool to lukewarm. Stir in the egg, then shortening and sugar, sourdough, and flour mixture. Add nuts last. Turn into prepared pan. Bake in moderate oven 350° for 25 minutes. Frost with Orange Frosting.

Orange Frosting
Beat 2 cups confectioners' sugar, 2 tablespoons orange juice and 1 tablespoon melted butter in a pan until smooth. Spread on squares, then cut.

Sourdough Spirited Raisin Cookies

1 cup raisins
½ cup warm rum
1 cup butter, softened
½ cup powdered sugar, sifted
2 cups flour
¼ teaspoon salt
¼ teaspoon baking powder
¼ cup sourdough starter

Bring raisins to a boil in the rum. Remove from heat. Cover and let stand 30 minutes. Drain. Cream butter and sugar, add sourdough. Sift flour with salt and baking powder, add to creamed mixture, add raisins. Roll out dough to ½ inch thick on floured board, cut with cutter. Bake at 375° F. for 20 minutes.

Sourdough Sugar Cookies

Blend ½ cup butter
½ cup shortening
1 cup sugar
½ cup sourdough starter
2 teaspoons vanilla OR
  1 teaspoon vanilla &
  1 teaspoon almond extract
1 egg
½ teaspoon salt
Blend in 2½ cups flour
2 large tablespoons of cream
  if needed

Mix in order as given. Roll into balls. Smash with a glass that has been dipped in sugar or roll and cut into shapes. Dust with colored sugar or sprinkle with nutmeg. (You may frost with a hard sauce).

Bake in 375° F. oven for 10 to 12 minutes.

My Mother's Sugar Cookies (Sourdough)

1 cup shortening
  (margerine or butter)
1 cup sugar
1 cup powdered sugar
2 eggs
1 cup oil
½ cup sourdough starter
4 cups flour (4½ cups
  if using pre-sifted flour)
1 teaspoon cream of tarter
½ teaspoon soda
1 teaspoon salt
2 teaspoons vanilla

Mix in order given. Chill dough. Roll into balls and press with glass dipped in sugar.

Bake 10 to 12 minutes at 350° F. on ungreased cookie sheet.

Sourdough Snooker Doodles

1 cup shortening
2 eggs
2 teaspoons cream of tarter
1 teaspoon salt
1½ cups white sugar
2¾ cups flour
1 teaspoon soda
⅓ cup sourdough starter

Mix all ingredients together. Make into balls and roll in 2 tablespoons sugar mixed with 1 tablespoon cinnamon. Flatten with bottom of glass.

Bake in 350° F. oven for 12 minutes or until done.

Sourdough English Walnut Cookies

2 cups brown sugar
1 cup shortening or ½ cup shortening and ½ cup butter
1 cup warm coffee
3 cups Gold Medal flour
1 teaspoon soda
½ cup starter
1 teaspoon salt
1 cup each, raisins and English walnuts, chopped
2 eggs
1 teaspoon nutmeg
1 teaspoon cinnamon

Cream shortening and sugar, sift all dry ingredients. Alternate dry and liquid ingredients. Starting with and ending with dry ingredients. Add raisins and walnuts last. Drop by teaspoons onto greased cookie sheet. Bake in moderate oven 350° F. for 10 minutes or until brown.

Sourdough Walnut Jumbos

Pre-heat oven to 350°
1 1/2 cups all-purpose Gold Medal flour
1/4 teaspoon salt
1/2 teaspoon baking powder
1/2 teaspoon soda
1/2 teaspoon ground cinnamon
1/2 teaspoon ground ginger
Sift 1st 6 ingredients together, set aside.
1/2 cup butter or margarine, softened
1 cup light or dark brown sugar
1 large egg
1 cup dark molasses
1/4 cup sourdough starter
2 cups uncooked quick oats
1 cup chopped walnuts

Preheat oven to 350°F. Lightly grease cookie sheets. Resift flour with salt, baking powder, soda and spices. In a large bowl beat butter, sugar and egg. Mix well. Blend in molasses, sourdough starter, then add flour (add 1/4 cup more if needed, dough should be slightly firm), add oats. Stir in 3/4 cup of the walnuts. Drop by quarter cupfuls onto slightly greased baking sheets, allowing room for spreading, flatten slightly. Sprinkle top with remaining nuts.

Bake above oven center for 13 to 15 minutes, until lightly brown. Let stand on sheets for 2 minutes and then remove to wire racks to cool. Makes 24 cookies. Approximately 195 calories per cookie.

Sourdough Crepes

2 cups sourdough starter
sponge (see note)
½ cup milk
1 teaspoon baking soda
½ teaspoon salt
1 teaspoon sugar
1 tablespoon melted butter
4 tablespoons butter for cooking

Note: Mix starter sponge the night before using 1½ cups flour, 1½ cups water, a dash of sugar and add the Mother Reserve. Mix and cover, let set overnight. Next morning take your Mother Reserve back out, cover with a teaspoon of sugar and return uncovered to the refrigerator for future use.

Mix all other ingredients together with leftover sponge. Let set for 5 minutes before cooking. Pour dough in center of skillet, preheated, and with plenty of butter to keep from sticking. Swivel skillet around so dough will be thin. Brown on both sides. Set on paper towels to cool.

These are wonderful served with strawberries and whipped cream. At our house we love them served as a desert with huckleberries and whipped cream. Blueberries and whipped cream are a nice treat for breakfast.

Asparagus Stuffed Crepes

1 lb. fresh asparagus spears
4 hardboiled eggs
4½ inch slices of
Monterey Jack Cheese
1 cup Sharp Cheddar cheese
1 cup medium white sauce

Cook asparagus until firm. Lay three sticks in a crepe. Top with hardboiled egg sliced thin, Jack Cheese, and cover with white sauce in which 1 cup of cheddar cheese has been added. Roll and put in a shallow pan. Cover with remaining cheddar cheese. Heat in 375° oven for 10 min.

White Sauce

Melt 1 tablespoon butter in skillet on medium heat. Add 3 teaspoons flour, stir well. Add 1 cup milk – cook until slightly thick. Add more milk if needed. Salt to taste.

Sourdough Crepes Filled With Ham

Sourdough Crepe Recipe

Filling:
1 tablespoon butter
½ lb. mushrooms, sliced
½ cup diced green onions
¼ cup chopped green pepper
1 cup diced ham, about 8 ozs.
2 hard cooked eggs, chopped
1 tablespoon minced fresh dill
¼ cup sour cream
2 teaspoons dijon mustard
5 to 6 tablespoons melted
butter, for cooking crepes
1½ cups grated Swiss cheese
Fresh dill for garnish

Melt butter in large skillet. Add mushrooms and cook until brown and liquid has evaporated. Remove and set aside on plate. Stir onions, green pepper and ham into skillet. Cook until pepper is crisp and tender, about 4 minutes. Stir in mushrooms and remove from heat. Stir in eggs, dill, sour cream and mustard.

Put about 1 tablespoon of filling into each crepe. Sprinkle with Swiss cheese and roll up. Repeat until all filling is used. Put into a large pan, sprinkle with remaining cheese over top, put into oven at 350° for 15 minutes. Serve.

Basic Recipe For Sourdough Muffins

In the evening before using, or 6 to 8 hours before using, set sponge by using 2 cups water, 2 cups flour and adding your Mother Reserve, mix well and let set overnight. Take your reserve back out and refrigerate for future use. Add to the remaining sponge:

1½ cups whole wheat flour
½ cup sugar
1 teaspoon salt
¼ cup non-fat dry milk
1 teaspoon soda
1 cup raisins (optional)
½ cup melted butter
1 or 2 eggs

Sift dry ingredients into a bowl. Make a well in the center. Mix egg and fat thoroughly with sourdough sponge. Add this to the flour mixture. Stir only to moisten the flour. Fill greased muffin tins ¾ full. Bake at 375° F. oven for 25 to 30 minutes or until done. Makes 12 large muffins.

Sourdough Apple Streusel Muffins

These muffins have a crumb topping that makes them resemble miniature coffee cakes. Been a favorite in our family for years.

Batter:
1½ cups all-purpose flour
½ cup sugar
2 teaspoons baking powder
1 teaspoon cinnamon
½ teaspoon soda
¼ teaspoon allspice
⅜ teaspoon salt
2 eggs
½ cup sourdough starter
1 cup sour cream
¼ cup melted butter
1 cup diced unpeeled
applies (tart)

Topping:
½ cup chopped walnuts
¼ cup all-purpose flour
3 tablespoons sugar
2 tablespoons butter at room temperature
½ teaspoon cinnamon

Mix flour, baking powder, sugar, soda, cinnamon, allspice, soda and salt together in a bowl until well blended. Mix eggs and sour cream, sourdough starter and melted butter. Beat until well blended. Stir in diced apples. Pour egg mixture over flour mixture and blend until dry ingredients are moist. Spoon into greased muffin tins. Top with cinnamon topping. Bake 375° F. for 20 minutes.

Topping:
Mix all ingredients with fork until mixture resembles coarse meal.

Sourdough Blueberry or Huckleberry Muffins

2 cups flour
1 tablespoon baking powder
¼ cup sugar
1 teaspoon salt
1 egg, slightly beaten
1 cup milk
½ cup sourdough starter
⅓ cup butter or oil, melted

Preheat oven to 400° F. (hot). Grease muffin tins.

Mix all dry ingredients thoroughly. Combine egg and milk; add butter, and sourdough starter. Add to dry ingredients. Stir until dry ingredients are barely moistened. Do not overmix. Batter should be lumpy. Lightly mix in the blueberries or huckleberries that have been dusted lightly with flour. Pour muffin tins half full of batter.

Bake 20 to 25 minutes until brown as desired.

Apple-Spice Muffins

Use ½ cup sugar and ¾ cup milk in the basic recipe. Add 1 teaspoon cinnamon to the dry ingredients, 1 cup finely grated apples and ¼ cup raisins with the liquid to the dry ingredients.

Sourdough Banana All-Bran Muffins

Set starter sponge the night before or dip from your starter pot ½ cup of starter sponge. Be sure to add back ½ cup water and ½ cup flour. If you dip from starter pot, let set at room temperature for 4 hours before returning to the refrigerator.

1 large egg
3/4 cup firmly packed dark brown sugar
1/3 cup peanut oil
1/2 cup starter sponge
1 1/2 cups mashed ripe bananas
1 teaspoon vanilla
2 cups All-Bran
1 1/2 cups all-purpose flour
2 teaspoons baking powder
1/4 teaspoon salt
1 teaspoon soda
1 teaspoon cinnamon
1/2 cup raisins
1/2 cup chopped walnuts
1 cup Raisin Bran soaked in 1 cup boiling water

Heat oven to 375° F. Grease regular size muffin tins.
In a medium sized bowl, beat the egg and sugar. Add bananas, sourdough sponge, vanilla, oil, raisins and walnuts. Beat until smooth. Let stand for a few minutes at room temperature. Thoroughly mix flour and all-bran, baking powder, salt, cinnamon and soda. Add to the banana mixture. Add the raisin bran that has been soaking in the boiling water. Stir just until all the ingredients are moistened. Spoon into muffin tins and bake for 20 minutes until brown and springy to touch.
This recipe will keep for two days in the refrigerator. Cook as needed.
These muffins are moist and after cooked will keep for one week in refrigerator. Makes 18 large muffins. 196 calories per muffin.

Sourdough Banana-Bran Muffins

These muffins are moist and perfect for breakfast.

1 larg egg
¾ cup packed light
  brown sugar
1⅓ cups mashed ripe bananas
½ cup raisins or chopped nuts
⅓ cup vegetable oil
1 teaspoon vanilla
¾ cup all-purpose flour
¾ cup whole-wheat flour
½ cup oat bran or
  unprocessed wheat bran
2 teaspoons baking powder
½ cup sourdough starter sponge
½ teaspoon soda
1 teaspoon cinnamon
1 teaspoon salt

Heat oven to 375° F. Grease 12 regular size muffin cups.

With a wooden spoon beat the egg and sugar in a medium size bowl until smooth. Add bananas, walnuts or raisins, oil and vanilla. Stir in the sourdough starter. Beat until well blended and let stand for 1 minute. Thoroughly mix flours, bran, baking powder, soda, cinnamon and salt in a large bowl. Add banana mixture and fold in with a spatula just until dry ingredients are moistened. Spoon into muffin cups and bake 20 minutes until brown and springy to touch.

Buttermilk Sourdough Refrigerator Bran Muffins

Note: Batter will keep six weeks if kept in refrigerator in a tightly closed jar.

1¼ cups sugar
½ cup plus 1½
  tablespoons shortening
2 eggs
2 cups buttermilk
1 cup sourdough starter
1 cup All Bran
1 cup boiling water
2 cups Bran Buds
3 cups flour
2½ teaspoons soda
1 teaspoon salt

Pour boiling water over All Bran and let set. Cream sugar and shortening. Beat in eggs. Add buttermilk and sourdough starter, All-Bran and water mixture. Now add all dry ingredients, stirring after each addition. Refrigerate as indicated.

When needed, fill greased muffin tins ⅔ full and let stand at room temperature for 10 to 15 minutes. Bake 16 to 19 minutes at 400°.

Sourdough Bran Refrigerator Muffins

1 cup flaked bran
1 cup boiling water
½ cup slightly softened
  butter or margerine
½ cup brown sugar
2 eggs
½ cup sourdough starter sponge
2 cups all bran cereal
2 cups buttermilk
2½ cups unbleached flour
2½ teaspoons baking soda
1 teaspoon salt

Put bran flakes in a small bowl and cover with boiling water. Let stand for 5 minutes. Meanwhile, cream the butter with the sugar. Beat in the eggs and sourdough starter. Stir in the buttermilk and bran cereal. Combine the flour, salt and soda. Add to the mixture of eggs along with the well-soaked bran flakes. Stir until well blended. Cover and store in the refrigerator until needed. Will last up to two weeks in the refrigerator.

To bake: Spoon into greased muffin cups and bake in a preheated oven 400° F. for 20 to 25 minutes. Makes 2½ dozen muffins.

Sourdough Bran-Pecan Muffins

2 cups all-purpose flour
2 tablespoons sugar
¼ teaspoon salt
1 teaspoon soda
½ cup sourdough starter sponge
2 tablespoons grated orange rind
1½ cups bran
⅔ cup chopped pecans
⅓ cup raisins
2 cups buttermilk
1 egg, well-beaten
½ cup dark molasses
3 tablespoons melted butter

Sift together flour, sugar, salt and soda. Add orange peel, bran, pecans and raisins and mix well. Beat together buttermilk, egg, molasses, sourdough starter and melted butter; add to flour mixture. Stir just enough to mix – a few fast strokes. Fill greased muffin tins about ¾ full and bake in preheated oven 350° F. for 25 to 30 minutes or until done. Cool 5 minutes before removing from pans.

Sourdough Cornmeal Muffins

1 cup flour, (unsifted)
plus 1 tablespoon
1 cup yellow cornmeal
1 tablespoon baking powder
1 cup sourdough starter
⅓ cup sugar
½ teaspoon salt
1 egg, well-beaten
1 cup milk
¼ cup melted butter

Preheat oven to 400° F. Grease muffin tins.

Mix all dry ingredients thoroughly. Combine egg, milk, sourdough starter, add butter. Add to dry ingredients and stir until dry ingredients are moistened. Do not over mix. Bake 20 minutes or until lightly browned.

Calories per muffin, about 160.

Sourdough English Muffins

The night before take your reserve starter from the refrigerator and add 2 cups water, 2 cups unbleached flour and 1 tablespoon sugar. Cover and let set overnight. Next morning take out your Mother Reserve and cover with a teaspoon sugar, return to the refrigerator.

2 cups sourdough starter
2 cups flour
1 teaspoon salt
2 tablespoons honey
about ¼ cup yellow cornmeal
3 tablespoons melted butter
or shortening

(continued next page)

If you have never made English Muffins they are as easy to make as other breads. They bake very slowly on a griddle or frying pan instead of the oven.

Mix the starter, melted butter, honey and salt together. Mix in the all-purpose unsifted flour. More flour may be added if needed. Turn out onto a floured board and knead until smooth. Place the dough in a greased bowl, turn over to grease top, cover and let rise in a warm place until double in size. About 2 hours. Punch dough down and turn onto a board lightly sprinkled with cornmeal. Roll out dough to about ½ inch thick. With a 3 inch cookie cutter (or a tuna can with both ends removed), cut dough in rounds. Place muffins, cornmeal side up about 1 inch apart on a baking sheet lightly sprinkled with cornmeal. Cover lightly and let rise until puffy but not doubled in size, about 60 minutes.

To bake muffins, preheat an electric griddle or fry pan to 275° F. Lightly grease surface and bake muffins slowly to golden brown. It should take 12 to 15 minutes on each side. Handle muffins carefully so they won't lose puffiness before becoming set. Split one muffin to test for doneness in center before removing the rest from the griddle. Cool on wire racks.

I was one of 11 children making 13 of us in the family. And always friends or neighbors would show up around supper time and be invited to stay. How would you like to bake enough bread to feed that kind of a group every day?

As a child I used to stand on a chair to dry the dishes and when Mother made the bread. When her hands became too "sticky" to dip the flour from the sack, I would do the dipping and add it to the bread as she called for it.

She made the dough in a large steel dish washing type pan. After kneading the dough the same pan was used for the bread to set and rise in. Covered with a damp cloth, the pan would be set in the sun to raise. If it was a cold day, the pan would be set on top of the warming oven on the "Old Wood Stove."

The kitchen was always very warm in the summer and yet so fresh and inviting, with the smell of cinnamon rolls and hot bread baking. I remember when, in later years, how embarrassed I was when I had to take homemade bread sandwiches in my lunch to school. All the other children had enticing store bought bread. Yet they would always want to trade lunches with me!

Boy, I always thought we were so poor because we couldn't afford store bought bread. Nonetheless, we were so rich and fortunate to have the most wonderful of all. Homemade bread.

Beignets

These square doughnuts are quick and easy to make. They do not have to raise before cooking. It is important to have the oil for frying very hot. 375° to 380°F. The quicker you cook them the better they are, and not tough on the outside.

Mix up enough starter the night before to make 2 cups of sponge.

Mix 1 cup of your Mother Reserve with 1 cup of water and 1 cup of flour. Mix well. Cover and let set over night. (Be sure to add 1/2 cup water and 1/2 cup flour back to your Reserve Pot.)

In a large skillet, put enough oil to make at least 1 1/2 inches.
Heat oil to 375°F.
To the 2 cups of starter sponge add:
1/4 cup dry milk
1 teaspoon salt
4 tablespoons melted butter
1 tablespoon honey
1 teaspoon vanilla
1 egg yolk
1 egg white, beaten very stiff
1/8 teaspoon cinnamon
dash of nutmeg
1 tablespoon baking powder
2 1/2 cups flour
Set aside 2 cups powdered sugar to dip beignet's in.

Mix the dry milk into the sponge, add salt, butter, honey, vanilla and egg yolk. Mix well. Gently fold in the well beaten egg white. Mix the flour with the spices and baking powder. Add to sponge. Mix well. Turn out onto a floured board and kneed slightly. Roll to 1/2 inch thick, cut into squares 3x3 inches. Add 4 of these at a time to the hot oil. Oil is hot enough when the beignets come to the top in 8 seconds. Baste with oil until golden brown on both sides. Drain well on paper towels. Dust with powdered sugar while still hot. Serve warm with coffee. Great with Chicory Coffee.

Approximately 155 calories each with powdered sugar.

Sourdough Waffles, Sourdough Hot Cakes and Sourdough Pudding

Sourdough Pancakes

3 cups sourdough starter sponge
1 egg
1 teaspoon baking soda
dash of baking powder
dash of salt
1 tablespoon melted butter
(optional)
1/4 - 1/2 cup milk

The night before take your Mother Reserve starter from the refrigerator. Add 2 cups water, 2 cups flour and 1 teaspoon sugar. Mix well, cover and let set overnight. The next morning take out your Mother Reserve and return to refrigerator for future use.

Heat grill. Mix the sourdough starter sponge, egg, salt and melted butter. Mix well. Add the soda last, right before cooking.

Blueberry Hotcakes:

Dust blueberries with flour. Add to the hotcake mix. Cook on 370° grill.

Huckleberry hotcakes:

Wash and clean fresh wild huckleberries. Pour hotcake batter onto grill. Sprinkle huckleberries on top of batter. Cook until bubbles form. Turn. Cook until done. Serve with fresh butter and real maple syrup.

Hot Cakes

When I was a small girl, growing up, I can remember making these every morning. We were a family of 11 children and did we eat!

Beat 6 eggs until foamy
Add ½ cup sugar
Add 3 heaping teaspoons
baking powder
½ teaspoon salt
1 quart of milk
1 cup sourdough starter
add flour to thickness desired

Cook on 375° grill.

When any of these hotcakes were left over they were rolled up with cinnamon and sugar and left on the warming oven on top of the wood cook stove to be eaten when anyone came in from chores, or home from school.

Sourdough Banana Pancakes

3 cups sourdough starter sponge
1 egg
1 teaspoon baking soda
dash of baking powder
dash of salt
1 tablespoon melted butter
 or bacon fat
1 cup mashed bananas
 (well ripened)

Set your starter the night before by the following method: Put 2 cups water into a glass bowl, add your Mother Reserve, 2 cups all-purpose flour and 1 teaspoon sugar. Mix well. Cover and let set overnight. Next morning take your Mother Reserve out and return to the refrigerator for future use.

For the hotcakes:

Heat grill to 375°

In the remaining sponge, add well beaten egg, salt and melted butter. Add the mashed bananas. Mix well. Add soda and dash of baking powder moments before ready to cook.

Pour 4-inch circles onto the grill. Cook until bubbles form on top. Turn, cook until done.

Serve with warm real maple syrup, huckleberry syrup or any of your favorite syrups.

Corn sourdough hotcakes

Make as above, only substitute 1 cup whole kernel corn or 1 cup of creamed corn for the bananas.

Sourdough Whole Wheat Hotcakes

The night before take ½ cup starter out of your Mother Reserve, (be sure to add the same amount of water and flour back to the pot.) In a medium bowl, add 1½ cups water, the ½ cup starter, 1 teaspoon sugar, and 1½ cups (more or less) of whole wheat flour. Mix thoroughly and let set overnight.

Next morning you may dip out a cup of the starter to set back into the refrigerator for a whole wheat start. Sprinkle a small amount of sugar on top before refrigerating.

Pancakes

1½ cups whole wheat sponge
1 teaspoon baking soda
small pinch of baking powder
¾ teaspoon salt
1 egg
1 tablespoon melted butter
or bacon grease

Mix and cook on hot grill at 375°. Serve with favorite berry syrup or maple syrup.

Sourdough Bread Pudding With Black Jack Daniel's Whiskey Sauce

Serves 8 to 10 people

Pudding:

2 tablespoons melted butter
1 16 ounce loaf homemade
sourdough bread, 1 or 2 days old
3 cups milk
4 eggs
1½ cups sugar
1 cup seedless raisins soaked in ½ cup
Black Jack Daniel Whiskey
2 tablespoons vanilla or seeds
scraped from one vanilla bean

Preheat oven to 350° F.

Spread the 2 tablespoons melted butter in a 9x13-inch baking dish. Break the bread into chunks, pour the milk over them and let set until the bread softens and all the milk is absorbed. Lightly squeeze bread, and pour off any excess milk. Add raisins and whiskey. Beat the eggs and sugar together until thick and lemon colored. Add vanilla. Pour over the bread crumbs and stir until all ingredients are well combined. Pour into the buttered dish. Spread evenly. Place the dish into a shallow pan, in the center of the oven. Pour 1-inch of boiling water into the shallow pan. Bake 1 hour or until a knife inserted comes out clean.

Whiskey Sauce:
½ pound of butter
2 cups sugar
2 eggs
½ cup whiskey

Prepare the sauce while the pudding is cooking.

Melt the butter in top of double boiler, over hot but not boiling water. Stir the sugar and eggs together in small bowl. Beat well. Add eggs to melted butter. Stir for 5 to 10 minutes until all sugar is melted completely and eggs are cooked. Do not let eggs come to a boil or the eggs will curdle. Remove from heat. Cool to room temperature before adding the whiskey. Serve pudding hot with whiskey sauce on the side.

You can make this sauce in the microwave oven: first melt butter, beat eggs and sugar together, add to butter. Cook in microwave for 3 minutes. Do not over-cook. Take out and set aside to cool. Add whiskey when cool.

Sourdough Strawberry Orange Banana Morning Coffee Cake

This recipe takes 45 to 50 minutes to cook and a few extra minutes to prepare. It is worth the time and effort. (The strawberries are folded in at the last minute.)

Move oven rack to one level above center.

Set oven to 350°F

Grease and flour one 8x13 inch baking dish or two nine inch round pans.

Dip out 3/4 cup of your Mother Reserve and let set at room temperature, set aside. Add 3/4 cup of water and 3/4 cup of flour back to your reserve for future use. (Let set at room temperature for 2 hours before returning to refrigerator.)

Mash 3 ripe bananas until very mushy (or enough for 1 cup of mashed bananas).

Squeeze enough fresh oranges to make 3/4 cup (approximately 1 1/2 oranges). Wash and cut up 12 large fresh strawberries, more if needed to make 1 cup of berries mashed or blended in blender. If blender is used do not over blend.

Set out measuring spoons, egg beater, spatula, vanilla, baking powder, baking soda, salt, mayonnaise, sugar and Softasilk cake flour.

Recipe:
½ cup mayonnaise
3 eggs
1 1/2 cups sugar
2 teaspoons vanilla
3/4 cups sourdough starter sponge
1 cup mashed bananas
3/4 cup fresh orange juice
2 1/2 cups cake flour
1 teaspoon soda
1 teaspoon baking powder
1/2 teaspoon salt
1 cup fresh mashed strawberries

Mix flour, soda, baking powder and salt. Shake through a wire strainer 3 times. Set aside.

In a large mixing bowl, mix the 1/2 cup mayonnaise, 3 eggs. Beat well. Add the 1 1/2 cups sugar and mix until smooth. Stir in the sourdough and vanilla. Add bananas. Gently fold in the bananas. Now add the cake flour alternately with the orange juice. Mix until blended. When blended, quickly fold in the strawberries and pour into the greased and floured cake pan.

Bake at 350°F for 45 to 50 minutes or until a wooden toothpick comes out clean. Set aside to cool.

Frost with Butter frosting.

Butter Frosting:

4 cups powder sugar
1/2 cup butter melted
1/2 cup heavy whipping cream
1 teaspoon vanilla

Mix until smooth. More cream may be added if needed. Frosting should be soft and easy to manage. Spread on cool cake and serve. Decorate with fresh strawberries.

Sourdough Waffles

To mix your starter, the night before mix 3 cups water, 3 cups flour, add starter and 2 tablespoons sugar. Mix with electric mixer or by hand until thoroughly mixed. Cover and let set overnight. Set back enough start for your Mother Reserve.

Waffles
3 cups starter sponge
¼ teaspoon baking powder
1 teaspoon baking soda
dash salt
2 egg yolks
2 egg whites, stiffly beaten
1 tablespoon melted butter or oil

Mix starter, baking powder, soda, salt, melted butter and egg yolks. Gently fold in beaten egg whites. Pour onto hot waffle iron. Makes 6 waffles.

You may add bacon bits, or any of your favorite goodies to this recipe. This recipe may be doubled or tripled.

Sourdough Whole Wheat Waffles

Using 1 cup of sourdough Mother Reserve starter, the night before mix 1 cup starter with 1½ cups water and 1½ cups whole wheat flour. Cover and let set overnight. Next morning add:

1 tablespoon firmly packed brown sugar
2 teaspoons baking powder
½ teaspoon salt
5 eggs, well-beaten
½ cup melted butter
¼ cup chopped pecans

Bake in a hot waffle iron until done.
Serve with fresh maple syrup or with whipped cream and strawberries.

FAVORITE RECIPES

Angel Food Cake

A Real American Favorite

Preheat oven to moderate 375° F. Place oven rack on lower third of oven.
For those of you that cannot handle preservatives, try the old-fashioned recipe.

1 cup sifted cake flour
(you can use all-purpose if it is sifted several times)
¾ cup granulated sugar
(or 1¼ cups sifted 10x confectioners' sugar)
1½ cups egg whites
(12 to 14 eggs) at room temperature
1½ teaspoons cream of tartar
¼ teaspoon salt
¾ cup granulated sugar
1 teaspoon vanilla
½ teaspoon almond extract

Combine sifted flour with the ¾ cup granulated sugar; sift three more times. Set aside.

Beat egg whites in a large bowl until foamy. Add cream of tartar, and salt; beat until soft peaks form. Gradually beat in the ¾ cup granulated sugar, 2 tablespoons at a time, until stiff peaks form. Add vanilla and almond extract.

Sift ¼ cup of the flour mixture at a time over the meringue; gently fold in after each addition. Turn into a 10x4-inch ungreased tube pan. Gently cut through batter with knife to prevent air pockets from forming.

Bake in lower half of preheated oven (375°) for 30 to 35 minutes. Remove cake immediately and invert pan, placing tube on bottle. Let cake cool in pan 2 hours.

To remove cake from pan, run sharp, thin knife around sides of pan. Remove outside rim. If you do not have this type of pan, tape the bottom gently on top of plate to remove. Dust crumbs from sides. Frost with favorite frosting.

New Bride's Cheesecake

1 cup graham cracker crumbs
2 tablespoons sugar
¼ cup melted butter
Dash of cinnamon

Mix crumbs and melted butter with the dash of cinnamon and sugar. Press into an 8-inch pie shell. Bake in 350° F oven for 10 minutes. Take out and set aside to cool.

Filling:
1 package of Jello Cheesecake mix
2 cups milk (or what the directions on package say)
1 package Dream Whip
13 ounces of cream cheese (Tuttle cream cheese if you can find it)

Put cheesecake mix into bowl. Add the Dream Whip and 2 cups milk. Beat until well blended. Add the softened cream cheese. Beat well until all cheese is mixed in and mix is smooth. Pour into chilled pie shell. Serve chilled.

Mrs. Larive's Rhubarb Cake

1 cup sugar
1 cup cream (sweet or sour)
1 egg
1 teaspoon soda
1½ cups flour
2 cups raw rhubarb,
cut into small pieces
Dash of salt

Mix all ingredients and pour into a greased and floured 9x13 pan. Bake for 40 minutes at 350° F.

Top with ⅔ cup of brown sugar and sprinkle chopped nuts on top.

Grandma's Sponge Cake

Weigh unbroken eggs; use same weight in sugar; use half same weight in flour; use 2 teaspoons of vinegar if one pound of eggs are used. To mix: separate eggs; beat yolks well. Add sugar gradually, beating well; stir in the flour (do not beat it in); add the vinegar; fold in the egg whites (beaten stiff). Bake in a 350° oven, time depending on the size of your cake. I found six (so called) large eggs weigh 1 pound, so I used 1 pound of sugar, ½ pound of flour, 2 teaspoons vinegar. It made a 10-inch angel cake size. Cake can be made to suit your needs. Either large or small, depending on the eggs.

Cookies

Skillet Cookies

Cube of butter, melted
4 tablespoons cocoa
Add 2 cups sugar
½ cup milk
½ cup peanut butter
3 cups quick oatmeal
1 teaspoon vanilla

Put butter, cocoa, sugar and milk in pan and boil. Bring to a good rough boil. Take off stove and add ½ cup peanut butter. Stir till melted, then add 1 teaspoon vanilla, 3 cups quick oatmeal. Let stand for 10 minutes in pan. Drop onto waxed paper to cool.

Cereal Chip Cookie Crunchies

1 package Bakers semi-sweet chocolate chips
1 package Bakers peanut butter flavor chips
2 tablespoons butter
4 cups Post Toastie Corn Flakes

Melt chips and butter together in the top of a double boiler. Pour over cereal and toss lightly to coat. Shape into mounds on waxed paper. Cool until firm. Cover and store in refrigerator. Makes 3 dozen clusters.

Rolled Chocolate Crispies

2 cups sifted all-purpose flour
½ teaspoon soda
½ cup shortening
¾ cup sugar
1 egg
2 tablespoons water
1 teaspoon vanilla
2 oz. unsweetened chocolate,
  melted and cooled
1 cup uncooked oatmeal

Sift flour, soda, and salt together into a bowl. Add shortening, sugar, egg, water, vanilla and chocolate. Beat until smooth, about 2 minutes. Beat in oats. Chill dough for 1 hour. Roll out on lightly floured board to ⅛ inch thick. Cut with cookie cutter. Place on ungreased cookied sheets and bake in 350° oven for 10 to 12 minutes.

Christmas Cookies

1 cup butter, softened
1½ cups powdered sugar
1 egg
1 teaspoon vanilla
2½ cups all-purpose flour

Cream butter, sugar, egg and vanilla thoroughly. Blend in flour. Roll dough out thinly on a floured board. Cut into your favorite shapes. Bake about 7 minutes on an ungreased cookie sheet in a preheated oven. 375°. Cool and frost or decorate with tinted frosting.

Frosting
2 cups powdered sugar
2 tablespoons butter
4 tablespoons milk or cream
1 teaspoon vanilla
Coloring of your choice

Chocolate Eclairs

Batter:
1 cup water
½ cup butter
¼ teaspoon salt
1 cup flour, sifted
4 eggs

Preheat oven to 425° F. Grease a large baking sheet. Heat water, butter and salt in a saucepan to a rolling boil. Stir in flour all at once. Reduce heat and continue stirring vigorously just until mixture leaves sides of pan and makes a ball-like mass. Remove from heat. Cool slightly. Beat in the eggs one at a time, until mixture is smooth. Shape the batter into 1-inch wide strips on baking sheet. Make 12 or 15 eclairs. Bake 35 to 40 minutes until browned and quite firm to the touch. Walls must be rigid to prevent collapse on removal from oven. Cool on rack.

Slice tops from cooled eclairs, and fill with cream pie filling. See below: Replace tops after filling and add chocolate glaze.

Vanilla Filling:
⅓ cup sugar
¼ cup cornstarch
½ teaspoon salt
2⅓ cups milk
3 egg yolks, beaten
2 tablespoons butter
1 teaspoon vanilla

Mix sugar, cornstarch, and salt in saucepan. Gradually stir in milk. Cook over moderate heat, stirring constantly, until thickened. Stir 1 minute longer.

Stir a little of the hot mixture into the beaten egg yolks; then stir yolks into remaining hot mixture. Cook 1 minute longer. Overcooking may thin the mixture. Remove from heat. Stir in butter and vanilla. Cool, pour into Eclairs. Pour chocolate sauce over top.

Chocolate Glaze for Eclairs:
1 ounce chocolate, unsweetened
1 tablespoon butter
2 tablespoons milk
1 tablespoon corn syrup
¼ teaspoon vanilla
1 cup confectioners' sugar

Melt chocolate and butter together over low heat; remove from heat. Add milk, corn syrup, and vanilla. Stir in confectioners' sugar and beat until smooth. Pour over top of eclairs.

Bananas Foster

4 small, ripe bananas
1 tablespoon lemon juice
⅔ cup brown sugar, packed
6 tablespoons butter
3 tablespoons banana liqueur
Vanilla ice cream
3 tablespoons light rum

Peel bananas and cut in half lengthwise; brush lightly with lemon juice.

In blazer pan or chafing dish, heat butter until melted. Add bananas and brown sugar. Cook 3 minutes, turning a few times. Add a dash of cinnamon to banana pan and sprinkle with banana liqueur. Have ice cream ready in individual serving dishes.

In a small saucepan heat rum just until you see waves in the liquid. Ignite with a match and pour over bananas. Spoon bananas over ice cream. Pour sauce over all. Serve immediately.

Banana Rum Fritters

6 firm bananas
½ cup rum
½ cup freshly squeezed orange juice
3 egg whites, slightly beaten
2 tablespoons cornstarch
2 tablespoons flour
¼ cup butter
¼ cup sugar

Peel bananas; cut in half lengthwise and then halve again. Place in a shallow dish. Pour the rum and orange juice over bananas. Let stand for half hour. In a small bowl mix egg whites, cornstarch and flour. Heat butter in large skillet. Take bananas from rum and orange juice (reserve juice). Dip bananas into egg white batter. Arrange in skillet with butter. Brown on all sides. Remove to a serving platter. Pour rum and orange juice sauce (the bananas had been marinating in) into skillet; add sugar; stir over high heat until sugar dissolves. Pour over bananas. Makes six servings.

Chocolate Rum Hot Fudge Pudding (For Microwave)

1 cup all-purpose flour
¾ cup sugar
3 tablespoons cocoa
2 teaspoons baking powder
½ teaspoon salt
½ cup milk
2 tablespoons butter, melted
1 teaspoon vanilla
⅔ cup chopped nuts
¾ cup packed light brown sugar
¼ cup cocoa
1 cup boiling water
¼ cup light or dark rum
Rum whipped cream

Combine flour, ¾ cup sugar, 3 tablespoons cocoa, baking powder, and salt in large mixing bowl. Stir in milk, butter, vanilla and half of the nuts. Spread batter in an 8-inch round or glass dish. Combine brown sugar, ¼ cup cocoa, remaining nuts, boiling water and rum in a small bowl. Pour over batter in dish. Do not stir! Cover dish with a paper towel. Microwave on high 9 to 11 minutes, rotating one-quarter turn halfway through cooking time. During baking cake rises to the surface and sauce forms in bottom. Let stand for 10 minutes before serving. Serve warm or cold with Rum Whipped Cream.

Rum Whipped Cream

Combine 1 cup heavy cream, 1 tablespoon rum and 2 tablespoons confectioners' sugar in a small bowl and beat until stiff peaks form.

To make pudding in a conventional oven: increase water to 1¼ cups and cook at 350° for 25 to 30 minutes.

Rum Chocolate Mousse

5 eggs
¼ cup coffee (or 2 tablespoons instant coffee dissolved in ¼ cup hot water)
¼ cup dark rum
¾ cup sugar
6 ounces semi-sweet chocolate
4½ ounces German chocolate
1½ sticks butter
Pinch of salt
Dash of cream of tartar (¼ teaspoon)

Separate the eggs. Beat the yolks in a glass bowl until thick and pale. In a pan, put coffee and sugar. Bring to a boil over moderate heat. Let boil until the sugar is dissolved. Now drizzle this sugar mixture over the beaten egg yolks, beating at moderate speed. Return this mixture to a double boiler and continue to beat for 5 minutes. But do not boil. Set aside while you melt the butter and chocolate, both semi-sweet and German, in a pan with the rum. Now drizzle the melted chocolate mixture over the egg mixture and rapidly fold until well blended. Set aside to cool. May be put over pan of cold water, to cool faster. While cooling, at once beat the egg whites with the cream of tartar, until stiff and glossy peaks form. Fold at once into the chocolate mixture, ¼ part at a time. Blend well. Put into glass serving bowls and chill for at least 2 hours before serving. May be made up to 2 days ahead. Keep refrigerated. Keeps up to 4 days in the refrigerator. May also be frozen. Serve with a topping of fresh whipped cream.

Suet Christmas Pudding

1½ cups seedless raisins
½ cup currants
1 tart apple, peeled, cored and grated fine
2 tablespoons grated lemon rind
2 tablespoons finely grated orange rind
1 cup rum or brandy (I prefer dark rum)
1 cup sifted flour
1 teaspoon baking powder or 1 teaspoon soda
½ teaspoon salt
1 teaspoon cinnamon
1 teaspoon allspice
1 teaspoon cloves
1 teaspoon nutmeg
1 cup fine dry sourdough bread crumbs
1 cup firmly packed dark brown sugar
½ cup dark molasses
1 cup finely ground suet (may substitute ½ cup melted butter)
3 eggs, lightly beaten

Mix fruits, rinds, and rum. Let stand half hour. Mix in brown sugar, molasses, eggs and suet or butter.

Sift together flour and spices, baking powder and salt. Add to fruit mixture and mix well. Add bread crumbs.

Spoon into 2 well-buttered 1 quart molds or metal bowls. Cover with a double thickness of foil and tie firmly in place. Set on rack in a large kettle and add boiling water to come halfway up on the molds. Cover and steam for 4 hours. Keep water simmering slowly and add more water as needed to maintain level. Cool puddings on racks with foil still intact. Store in a cool place, freeze or refrigerate.

To reheat, steam 1 hour. Unmold on hot platter. Decorate with holly or candied cherries. Pour ¼ cup brandy over and light. Serve when blaze is hot. Serve with a brandy or rum hard sauce.

Rice Pudding With Meringue

1⅓ cups water
½ cup uncooked rice
¾ teaspoon salt
3 eggs, yolks and whites, separated
½ cup granulated sugar
2 tablespoons cornstarch
¼ cup butter
2½ cups milk
1 teaspoon vanilla
¼ teaspoon almond extract
6 tablespoons sugar

Bring water to a boil in a medium saucepan; add rice and ½ teaspoon of the salt. Bring back to a boil. Reduce heat to low, cover pot and cook for 20 minutes until rice is tender and water is absorbed. Heat oven to 350° F. In a 1½ quart ovenproof casserole, beat the egg yolks with the remaining ¼ teaspoon of salt, the ½ cup sugar and the cornstarch. Stir in the butter, milk, almond and vanilla extracts and then add the cooked rice. Place casserole in a larger pan and fill larger pan with hot water to come to one inch of rim of casserole. Put in oven and bake 1 hour (350°). Stir 2 or 3 times during cooking time. In a medium sized bowl, whip egg whites until soft peaks form when beater is lifted; add remaining sugar 2 teaspoons at a time, beating well after each addition. When meringue is stiff and glossy, spoon it on top of the rice. Bake 10 to 15 minutes longer, until meringue is golden. Let cool at room temperature 1 to 2 hours before serving.

Southern Indian Pudding

½ cup Quaker Enriched Quick Grits
¼ teaspoon salt
2 cups water
1 tablespoon butter
3 eggs, beaten
1⅓ cups milk
1 teaspoon vanilla
1 teaspoon cinnamon
¼ cup raisins
¼ cup chopped almonds

Prepare grits in salted boiling water as directed on package. Stir in butter. Add combined eggs, milk, vanilla and cinnamon to grit mixture. Pour into greased 8-inch baking dish; sprinkle with raisins and almonds. Bake in preheated oven 325° for about 50 minutes. Cut into squares; serve warm or cold. Garnish with whipped cream, if desired.

Barbecue Sauce

1 bottle catsup
2 beef bouillon cubes,
  dissolved in 1 cup hot water
1 teaspoon salt
1 tablespoon Worcestershire sauce
4 cloves garlic
½ cup tarragon vinegar
⅛ teaspoon black pepper
½ teaspoon chili powder
½ cup brown sugar

Cook over low heat for 1 hour. Remove garlic before using with meat. Very good with spareribs, beef shortribs, and chicken.

Barbecue Sauce

½ cup fresh lemon juice
½ cup soy sauce
4 cloves garlic, finely chopped

Mix together and let set covered overnight to let the garlic flavor the sauce.

Brush over chicken, turkey and wonderful to pour over shrimp and let set for an hour before barbecuing. This is also very good on spare ribs.

Perfect Summer Barbecue Sauce

(Andy Anderson's)

Use 4 to 5 slices bacon for fat
(discard bacon)
1 bud garlic, whole bud diced
Add 4 small cans tomato paste,
rinse can with water
Add 2 small cans dry mustard or
1 large 4-ounce bottle
Trader Vic's Hot Mustard
½ cup pure maple syrup
(the real thing)
1 cup vinegar
1 bottle Louisiana Hot Sauce
10 ounce bottle Worcestershire sauce

Cook all together for 2½ hours. Add water if it gets too thick.

Brandy Custard Sauce

Lightly beat 3 egg yolks. Stir in 1¼ cups light cream or half-and-half, then add 3 tablespoons sugar, 1 teaspoon cornstarch and a pinch of salt. Cook mixture until thickens in the top of a double boiler. Remove from heat and stir in 2 tablespoons brandy and ½ teaspoon vanilla. Chill before serving. This sauce is excellent over bread pudding or plain cakes.

Cheese Sauce

This is good served over asparagus, broccoli, or any of your favorite dishes.

¼ cup butter
¼ cup flour
½ teaspoon salt
¼ teaspoon pepper
2 cups milk
½ teaspoon dry mustard
1 cup shredded sharp Cheddar cheese

In saucepan, melt butter over low heat. Blend in flour, salt, and pepper. Cook over low heat, stirring until mixture is smooth and bubbly. Remove and stir in milk. Heat until almost boiling. Cook stirring for 3 minutes. Stir in mustard and cheese. Heat over low heat until cheese is melted.

Hot Salsa

1 or 2 onions, chopped fine
1 large can whole tomatoes,
  or 4 ripe ones, chopped
4 jalapeno peppers, chopped fine
  (more or less to suit taste)
1 tablespoon vinegar
1 tablespoon oil
Salt to taste

Mix well, keep in refrigerator.

Hard Sauce

Cream well ½ cup sweet butter. Gradually beat in 1½ cups powdered sugar. Add 3 tablespoons brandy or rum or any liqueur — singly or in combinations to taste. Roll out in long rolls and wrap in foil. Cut slices as desired.

Brandied Hard Sauce

⅔ cup butter, softened
¼ teaspoon nutmeg
2 cups sifted powdered sugar
2 tablespoons brandy or rum

Combine butter and nutmeg. Blend well. Add sugar alternately with brandy or rum and blend well. Makes 1½ cups. Put into dish and serve with Christmas Pudding.

This may be made up a couple of days ahead and kept in the refrigerator. Keeps up to 3 weeks.

Raisin Rum Sauce

½ cup golden raisins, seedless
Hot water
½ cup light rum
⅓ cup sugar
2 tablespoons red currant jelly
1 teaspoon lemon juice

Cover raisins with hot water; let stand 5 minutes. Drain well. Combine raisins and rum. Let stand 30 minutes. Drain, reserving the rum. In saucepan heat to boiling 1 cup water and the sugar. Reduce heat; simmer 15 minutes. Stir in the jelly. Add raisins; simmer until plump, about 15 minutes. Remove from heat; stir in reserved rum and lemon juice. Makes about 2 cups. Very good served over custards.

Pies

Chocolate Fudge Pie

1 9-inch unbaked pie shell (see note)
¼ cup butter
¾ cup firmly packed brown sugar
3 eggs
1 12-ounce package semi-sweet
    chocolate pieces, melted
2 ounces German chocolate, melted
2 tablespoons strong coffee
1 tablespoon rum extract or
    3 tablespoons dark rum (if dark
    rum
    is used add 1 tablespoon
    more of flour)
¼ cup flour
1 cup coarsely broken walnuts
½ cup walnut halves for decoration

Cream butter with sugar, beat in eggs, one at a time. Add melted chocolate, coffee and rum. Stir in flour and broken walnuts. Turn into the unbaked pie shell. Top with the walnut halves. Bake at 375° F for 30 minutes. Cool. Serve with whipped cream. Makes 8 servings. This is also very good without the walnuts. Walnuts used only for top decoration.

Note: Pastry to make one 9-inch pie crust.
1¼ cups all-purpose flour
4 tablespoons chilled vegetable shortening or lard
2 tablespoons chilled butter, cut into small pieces
⅛ teaspoon salt
3 tablespoons ice cold water

In a large bowl add flour, salt, shortening and butter. Mix until the flour resembles a coarse meal. Add water and press together into a ball. Roll out and place into a 9-inch pie dish.

It always seems that a ghost has been in our house when I make this pie. Pieces just seem to disappear right in front of my face.

Grapefruit Meringue Pie

6 tablespoons cornstarch
1¼ cups sugar
¼ teaspoon salt
½ cup cold water
2 cups fresh grapefruit juice
3 egg yolks
1 teaspoon grated grapefruit rind
1 tablespoon butter
1 baked 8-inch pie shell

Mix cornstarch, sugar and salt in a large pan. Stir in water and grapefruit juice. Cook over medium heat, stirring constantly, until mixture comes to a boil. Continue to boil for 5 minutes. Remove from heat. In a small bowl, beat the egg yolks until lemon colored. Gradually stir in a small amount of hot grapefruit mixture. Then stir egg yolk mixture into the remaining hot mixture. Add rind and butter. Cool 10 minutes. Turn into pie shell. Top with meringue. Bake in 350° oven for 12 to 15 minutes.

Meringue
3 egg whites
¼ teaspoon cream of tartar
6 tablespoons sugar

Beat until very stiff peaks.

Glazed Strawberry Pie

1 baked 9-inch pie crust
1 quart plus 1 cup of strawberries
¾ cup sugar
2½ tablespoons cornstarch
¼ teaspoon salt
1 cup water

Clean and hull the strawberries. Take 1 cup of the berries and mash through a sieve. Put the 1 cup water, cornstarch and salt on a burner on low heat and stir until thickened (10 to 15 minutes). Add the blended strawberries that you just ran through the sieve.

Put whole berries in the pie shell (4 cups). Now pour the thickened syrup over the top until well coated. Turn softly but do not displace them. Chill and serve with whipped cream.

Note: If the strawberries are very large, you may want to slice some of them.

I have never had a bad strawberry pie from this recipe. It is beautiful to serve.

Gooseberry Pie

1 pie crust for a double-crusted pie
4 cups gooseberries
Dash of salt
¾ cup sugar
1 tablespoon flour
3 tablespoons water

Mix sugar and flour. Add to 2 cups gooseberries with the 3 tablespoons water. Put into saucepan and heat until the berries break. Remove from heat. Add 2 more cups gooseberries, pour into uncooked pie shell. Cover with another shell. Cook in 350° oven for 1 hour.

Heavenly Angel Lemon Pie

Meringue Crust:
1 cup granulated sugar
¼ teaspoon cream of tartar
4 egg whites

Start oven at 275°. Sift sugar and cream of tartar. With electric mixer or egg beater, beat egg whites until stiff but not dry. Slowly add sugar mixture, beating meringue until it makes stiff, glossy peaks.

Spread over bottom and sides just to the brim of a well-greased 9-inch pie plate. Have bottom covered to ¼ inch thickness and sides 1 inch thick. Bake about 1 hour or until light brown and crisp to touch. Cool away from draft. It is okay if it falls in the center.

Filling:
4 egg yolks (8 may be used)
½ cup granulated sugar
½ cup lemon juice
⅛ teaspoon salt
2 cups heavy cream

In a double boiler top, beat egg yolks slightly. Stir in sugar and lemon juice. Cook over boiling water, stirring 8 to 10 minutes or until thick. Let cool. Whip 1 cup cream, fold into lemon filling and pour into crust. Place into refrigerator for 12 to 24 hours. Serve with whipped cream.

Huckleberry Pie

1 cup huckleberries
1 cup water
1 cup sugar
3 tablespoons cornstarch
Dash of butter
Juice from ½ lemon or lime
3 to 4 more cups huckleberries
Pastry for 2 9-inch pie crusts

Mix sugar and cornstarch together. Put water, sugar and cornstarch plus the 1 cup of huckleberries in a pan over medium heat and cook until thick, stirring constantly. When thick, set aside and add the dash of butter and the lemon or lime juice. When slightly cool add the 3 to 4 cups more of huckleberries (4 cups for a nice thick pie). Put into an uncooked pie shell and cover with another crust. Make fork holes in top of crust. Pat with cool water and sprinkle with a small amount of sugar.

Bake 450° F for 10 minutes, then reduce heat to 350° F and cook for an additional 30 minutes. Cool completely before serving.

Blueberry Pie

Just substitute blueberries for the huckleberries.

Key Lime Mousse Pie

To make one 9-inch pie.

1 fully baked pie shell (see note)
6 egg yolks
½ cup sugar
¾ cup fresh juice from key limes
    (fresh limes will do as well)
6 egg whites
1½ tablespoons cornstarch

Preheat oven to 350°. With an electric beater, beat the egg yolks until lemon colored, add the sugar, beat for another minute. Add half of the lime juice. Transfer to a double-boiler and cook over low heat until mixture starts to thicken, add the other half of the lime juice that has been mixed with the cornstarch. Cook until thick. Cool slightly. Beat the egg whites until very thick. A little at a time fold them into the lime mixture. Pour into the baked pie shell and cook in the center of the oven for 5 to 10 minutes or until slightly browned. Chill and serve.

Pie Crust
1¼ cups all-purpose flour
4 tablespoons chilled Crisco
2 tablespoons butter, chilled and cut into small pieces
Dash of salt
Ice water (about ¼ cup)

In a large mixing bowl put flour, salt, Crisco and butter. Mix together with a pastry blender or use your fingers, until the flour, butter and Crisco look like flakes of fine meal. Add the water a little at a time. Dough should hold together when gathered into a ball. Roll and line a 9-inch pan and bake in a preheated oven 400° for 20 minutes or until done. Cool before filling.

Never Fail Pumpkin Pie

This recipe is for 2 8-inch pies.

2 pastry shells for 2 8-inch pies
1 large can of Libby's
Solid Pack Pumpkin
1½ cups sugar
1 teaspoon salt
2 teaspoons cinnamon
1 teaspoon ginger
½ teaspoon cloves
1 can Carnation evaporated milk
4 eggs, well beaten

Mix pumpkin, eggs, sugar and milk. Add salt and spices. Beat with electric mixer until well blended. About 3 minutes. Pour into uncooked pie shells. Bake in preheated oven 425° F for 15 minutes. Reduce temperature to 350° F and continue to bake for 45 minutes or until a knife inserted comes out clean.

Rum Banana Cream Pie

1 9-inch pie crust
½ cup sugar
5 tablespoons flour
Dash of salt
5 egg yolks
2 cups milk
2 tablespoons butter
1 teaspoon vanilla
¼ cup dark rum
1½ cups heavy whipping cream
4 large bananas, sliced into rounds

Sift the sugar and flour into a large bowl. With a beater, beat in the egg yolks one at a time. Beat until light and creamy. Heat the 2 cups of milk and the 2 tablespoons of the butter until the butter melts. Slowly pour the egg mixture into the milk, stirring constantly. Add the vanilla and the rum. Cook on low heat until sauce thickens to a smooth, heavy custard. Let it cool to lukewarm. Beat ½ cup of the cream and fold gently into the cool custard. Spread one layer of bananas in the bottom of pie shell, cover with custard, continue to put layer of bananas, layer of custard until full, leaving a layer of bananas on top. Beat remaining cream until stiff. Pile on top of pie. Chill for at least one hour before serving.

Rose's Rhubarb Cream Pie

(Rose Konola)

Pie crust for a double crust pie
3 cups rhubarb, cut up into 1-inch pieces

Mix together:
1½ cups sugar
2 large eggs
3 tablespoons flour
Dash of nutmeg

Pour over the rhubarb that has been put into an uncooked pie shell. Dot the top of rhubarb with two teaspoons butter. Top with crust. Wipe the top of crust with milk and sprinkle with sugar.

Bake at 400° F for 10 minutes, then turn heat down to 350° F and bake for 50 minutes more or until browned.

Strawberry Eggnog Pie

Makes 1 9-inch pie.

1 baked pie shell
1 envelope unflavored gelatin
⅛ teaspoon salt
½ cup sugar
1 cup cream
3 eggs, separated
2 tablespoons each dark rum and brandy
¼ teaspoon nutmeg
1 pint fresh strawberries

In a medium saucepan, mix gelatin with salt and ¼ cup of the sugar. Stir in cream. Beat egg yolks slightly and stir in. Cook, stirring constantly, until the mixture is thick enough to coat a metal spoon. Cool, then mix in rum and brandy. Stir in nutmeg. Chill mixture until thick enough to hold mounds. Meanwhile, beat egg whites until foamy, gradually adding the rest of the sugar; beating until stiff. Fold the egg whites into the egg yolk mixture. Spread small amount onto the bottom of pie shell. Slice the berries over filling, cover the berries with the remaining filling. Decorate with a few whole berries. Chill until set. Serve.

Baked Pastry Shell

Double recipe for double pie crust.

8 or 9-inch pie plate
1 cup flour, unsifted
½ teaspoon salt
⅓ cup shortening or lard
About 2 tablespoons or more
of cold water

Preheat oven to 450° F. Mix flour and salt thoroughly. Mix in fat with a pastry blender or two knives until mixture is crumbly. Add a little water at a time while blending lightly. Dough should be just moist enough to cling together when pressed.

For easier handling, cover and let set a few minutes in the refrigerator. Shape dough into ball. Roll out on a lightly floured board until the dough is at least an inch wider all around than the pie pan. Fold dough in half for easier lifting and centering in pie pan.

Smooth pastry into place. Trim off irregular edges leaving one-half inch beyond edge of pan, fold under to edge of pan. Shape edge into plain or fancy rim, as desired. Prick bottom and sides well with a fork before baking (for cream pies).

Bake 12 to 15 minutes until golden brown. Cool before filling.

Graham Cracker Pie Crust

11 double graham crackers, rolled
and crushed with a rolling pin
⅓ cup melted butter
¼ cup granulated sugar

Mix well and press into an 8-inch pie pan.
Bake slightly for 10 minutes at 350° F.

Oil Pie Pastry

Makes enough for one double crust pie (9-inch).

2 cups all-purpose flour
1 teaspoon salt
⅓ cup corn or other polyunsaturated oil
3 teaspoons cold skim milk

Sift flour and salt together in mixing bowl. Make a well in center. Mix oil and cold milk in a small bowl. Pour all at once into the well. Stir lightly with a fork until blended; add more milk if necessary to make dough hold together in a ball. Divide in half. Refrigerate a few minutes to rest dough. Use as you would any pie pastry.

Carrot Cake Frosting

6 oz. Philadelphia cream cheese
1 stick butter
1 teaspoon vanilla
3 cups powdered sugar

Whip with mixer, if needed add a little more powdered sugar or thick cream. Add chopped nuts on top if desired.

Miracle Cake Icing

1⅓ cups sugar
2 unbeaten egg whites
⅓ cup hot water
⅛ teaspoon salt
¼ teaspoon cream of tartar
1 teaspoon vanilla

Mix sugar, water and salt. Bring to a boil. Cover pan, turn off heat, cook for 3 minutes. Place unbeaten egg whites and cream of tartar in a small mixing bowl. Beat on high speed of electric beater for 5 minutes adding syrup a little at a time as you beat. Add vanilla. Spread on cake. This is a soft frosting, does not become crusty over the top. You may add 6 marshmallows to hot syrup, allow to dissolve before adding to egg white. Sufficient to frost 3 8-inch cakes or 2 9-inch layer cakes.

Ornamental Frosting

1¼ cups confectioner's sugar
⅛ teaspoon cream of tartar
1 egg white
½ teaspoon vanilla

Sift sugar and cream of tartar together. Add egg white and vanilla. Beat with rotary beater until frosting holds its shape.

This recipe can be doubled for large cakes.

Seven-Minute Maple Frosting

Yield: Frosting for 1 9-inch layer cake.

¾ cup maple syrup
¼ cup sugar
1 egg white
1 teaspoon light corn syrup
⅛ teaspoon salt

Place all of the ingredients in the top of the double boiler. Beat the mixture for 1 minute with an electric mixer.

Place the mixture over boiling water and cook it, beating constantly, until it is stiff enough to stand in peaks (about 7 minutes). Keep the water in the double boiler boiling actively throughout and scrape the mixture from the sides of the pan with a rubber spatula several times during cooking.

Remove the frosting from the heat and continue to beat until it is cool enough to spread.

Seven-Minute Frosting

Bring 1½ cups Log Cabin Syrup, any flavor, to a boil over direct heat in the top of a double boiler; boil 3 minutes. Cool. Add 2 egg whites and a dash of salt; beat until well blended, about one minute. Place over boiling water and beat at high speed on electric mixer for about 7 minutes, or until frosting will stand up in stiff peaks. Remove from heat and transfer at once to a large bowl and add 1 teaspoon vanilla and beat 1 more minute. Fill and frost 2 cooled, baked 8-inch cake layers.

Salads

Avocado Shrimp Treat

2 egg yolks
½ teaspoon mustard
Pinch of cayenne pepper or
  a dash of Tabasco sauce
½ teaspoon salt
1 teaspoon lemon juice
1 tablespoon white wine vinegar
1 cup salad oil
2 tablespoons catsup, or tomato puree
1 tablespoon cognac
1 pound medium cooked
  and peeled shrimp
3 avocados, halved and seeded,
  may leave with skins or may peel

To make cognac mayonnaise, put egg yolks, mustard, cayenne, salt, lemon juice and wine vinegar into a bowl and beat until thickened. Beat in the oil drop by drop until the mixture is very thick, then beat in the remaining oil in a steady stream. Add the catsup and cognac.

Arrange shrimp in avocado shells. Spoon mayonnaise on top. Serve.

Cinnamon Applesauce Salad

2 3-oz. packages Jello
  brand orange jello
1¾ cups boiling water
¾ cups cold water
1 cup applesauce
1 cup (8 oz.) sour cream
¼ teaspoon cinnamon
Nuts if desired

Dissolve 1 package of Jello in 1 cup boiling water, stir in the cold water. Chill until firm but not set.

Meanwhile dissolve remaining Jello in ¼ cup boiling water. Blend in the applesauce, sour cream and cinnamon. Chill until mixture starts to thicken. Spoon into mold all of the Jello mixture. Chill about 3 hours. Unmold and garnish with salad greens.

Frozen Cabbage Salad

1 small head cabbage
1 carrot
1 green pepper
1 teaspoon salt

Shred cabbage, add salt. Let stand for 1 hour. Drain off liquid. Add carrot, shredded or finely chopped, and green pepper, finely chopped.

Dressing:
1 cup vinegar
¼ cup water
1 teaspoon mustard seed
1 teaspoon celery seed
2 cups sugar
⅛ cup vegetable oil

Mix and boil for 1 minute. Cool to lukewarm, pour over cabbage. Put in jars and freeze.

Chicken Curry Layered Salad

6 cups shredded lettuce
2 10-oz. packages frozen peas,
  cooked, drained and chilled
3 cups chopped, cooked
  chicken or turkey
3 cups chopped tomatoes
2 cups seeded cucumber slices, halved
3 cups mayonnaise
1 tablespoon sugar
1½ teaspoons curry powder
3 cups croutons

Layer lettuce, peas, chicken, tomatoes, and cucumber in 5-quart salad bowl.

Combine mayonnaise, sugar and curry; mix well. Spread over salad. Cover with plastic film, refrigerate overnight. Before serving sprinkle with croutons.

Corned Beef Salad

1 package lemon jello
1¾ cup water
2 tablespoons white vinegar

Blend these 3 ingredients and let set enough to whip. Whip. Add:

½ cup corned beef, chopped
3 boiled eggs, sliced
1 cup celery, diced
⅓ (scant) cup bell peppers, chopped
1 teaspoon minced onion
1 cup mayonnaise

Blend all these ingredients in Jello. Set in refrigerator. When set serve on plate garnished with crisp lettuce leaves.

Cranberry Sauce

1 cup orange juice, freshly squeezed
1 cup sugar
1 12-ounce package cranberries
1 package unflavored gelatin

Put gelatin into orange juice to dissolve. Add sugar. Wash and pick over cranberries. Put into saucepan, add sugar and orange mixture. Cook for 10 minutes. When cranberries come to a full boil turn down heat, and cook at a slow simmer. Pour into mold. Chill.

Cucumbers in Sour Cream

½ clove garlic, crushed
¾ teaspoon salt
1½ cups sour cream
2 tablespoons fresh lemon juice
Dash pepper, freshly ground
2 medium cucumbers, peeled
  and sliced

Finely chop the garlic in salt, combine in a bowl with sour cream, lemon juice and pepper. Mix well and add the cucumbers and toss lightly. Chill and serve.

Egg Salad

6 chopped hard-cooked eggs
¼ cup finely chopped ripe olives
Salt to taste
Pepper to taste
2 teaspoons prepared mustard
½ cup mayonnaise or cooked salad
  dressing

Mix all ingredients together. Refrigerate. You may substitute 2 small dill pickles, grated, for the ripe olives.

Makes 2 cups filling for sandwiches.

Baked Potato Salad

1 cup chicken broth or bouillon
¼ cup olive oil
2 tablespoons cider vinegar
¼ cup finely chopped onions
2 teaspoons thyme leaves or
    celery seed, crushed
1 clove garlic, crushed
Salt to taste
¼ teaspoon freshly ground
    black pepper
2 pounds small red potatoes,
    cut into quarters

Preheat oven to 350°. Combine chicken broth, oil, vinegar, onion, thyme, garlic, salt and pepper.

Place potatoes in a shallow 3-quart casserole. Pour seasoned broth over all, tossing to coat.

Bake uncovered, until potatoes are fork tender, 35 to 40 minutes, stirring occasionally. Serve at room temperature on lettuce leaves if desired.

Hot Potato Salad

(Warmer Kartoffelsalat)

6 medium white potatoes
    (or 15 new red potatoes)
6 slices bacon, diced
½ cup sliced green onions
2 teaspoons sugar
1 teaspoon flour
1 teaspoon salt
⅛ teaspoon pepper
3 tablespoons white wine
2 teaspoons vinegar
½ cup water
¼ cup sliced green onion tops

Cook potatoes in boiling salted water until tender. Drain, peel and dice. Meanwhile, fry the bacon until crisp, remove from pan. Saute onion in the drippings until tender, but not browned. Drain off all but about 1 tablespoon of the drippings. Stir in sugar, flour, salt and pepper; then stir in the wine, water and vinegar. Cook and stir over medium heat until thickened. Mix with potatoes and bacon. Sprinkle with the green onion tops. Serve at once.

Summer Potato Salad

10 medium red potatoes (cooked, peeled and diced)
15 medium sized radishes, 12 for salad and 3 for garnish
¾ cup chopped green onions, tops included
½ cup grated Kosher style dill pickle
7 hard boiled eggs (grate 5 for salad, save 2 for garnish)
¼ teaspoon curry powder
¼ teaspoon ground basil leaves
¼ teaspoon paprika
¼ teaspoon salt or salt to taste
1 tablespoon prepared mustard
¾ cup Real mayonnaise

Mix diced potatoes, sliced radishes, chopped onions, grated pickle and grated eggs together in a large bowl. Add spices and mustard. Mix. Add mayonnaise and mix well. Mayonnaise will depend on how moist you want your salad. More or less may be used. Put into serving bowl. Cover top with slices of radishes and slices of eggs. Sprinkle with a small amount of paprika. Cover and set into refrigerator for at least 2 hours before serving.

Seven-Layer Salad

½ medium head iceberg lettuce, shredded
½ cup coarsely chopped celery
½ cup coarsely chopped red or green pepper
¾ cup coarsely chopped Spanish onion
½ 10-oz. package frozen peas, cooked and drained
1 cup mayonnaise
1 tablespoon sugar
1½ cups coarsely shredded mild or sharp Cheddar cheese
4 strips bacon, crisp-cooked and chopped

In a large salad bowl, arrange lettuce, celery, peppers, onions, and peas in layers. Spread mayonnaise evenly over peas. Sprinkle with sugar, then with Cheddar cheese. Cover and refrigerate at least 4 hours or overnight. Sprinkle with bacon bits before serving.

Day Ahead Spinach Salad

¾ pound spinach
1 medium sized cucumber, thinly sliced
½ cup thinly sliced radishes
½ cup thinly sliced green onions
3 hard-cooked eggs
¾ cup Roquefort dressing
6 slices bacon, crisply fried and crumbled

Discard spinach stems; rinse leaves well, drain and pat dry. Tear spinach into bite-size pieces and arrange evenly in shallow salad bowl. Then evenly layer cucumber slices, radishes, green onion and eggs. Spread dressing evenly on top, cover and chill as long as 24 hours. Just before serving, sprinkle with bacon bits. With a spoon and fork lift out each serving; be sure you get some of each layer of salad. See Roquefort Dressing, page 138.

Hot Spinach Salad

(Basic recipe makes 6 servings.)

2 quarts torn spinach, stems removed (10 oz.)
½ cup chopped green onion
1 cup cherry tomatoes, halved
2 tablespoons sugar
½ teaspoon salt
¼ teaspoon dry mustard
2 tablespoons lemon juice
1 tablespoon red wine vinegar
1 tablespoon catsup
½ teaspoon Worcestershire sauce
6 slices bacon, chopped

Range top cooking time 7 to 9 minutes.

Combine spinach, onion and tomato halves in salad bowl.

Stir together sugar, salt and mustard. Add lemon juice, red wine vinegar, catsup and Worcestershire sauce to the sugar mixture. Cook bacon in skillet 6 to 8 minutes or until crisp. Drain bacon on paper towels; set aside. Pour off all but 5 tablespoons bacon drippings.

Add lemon juice mixture to skillet. Bring to a boil, crumble bacon into spinach mixture. Pour hot dressing over all, toss and serve at once.

Garnish with hard-boiled eggs.

Wilted Spinach Salad

½ lb. fresh spinach
1 green onion and some of the tops, sliced
3 slices bacon, diced
1 tablespoon red wine vinegar
1½ teaspoons lemon juice
½ teaspoon sugar
Salt and pepper to taste
1 hard-cooked egg, peeled and chopped
Croutons to taste

Wash spinach and tear into bite-sized pieces. Mix with onion. Chill until serving time. Just before serving, fry bacon until crisp in a large skillet. Remove and drain on paper towel. To the bacon drippings add vinegar, lemon juice, sugar, salt and pepper. Cook until sugar dissolves. Add spinach and cook tossing continually until spinach is slightly wilted. Add egg and croutons. Toss again. Serve while hot.

You may substitute wine for vinegar — omit the lemon juice.

Add chopped radishes for color.

Sour Cream Salad

1 can mandarin oranges, well drained
1 can chunk or tidbit pineapple, well drained
1 cup angel flake coconut
12 large marshmallows cut 4 ways
1 package sour cream (1 pt.)

Mix well together and let set at least 24 hours. Great for potluck suppers.

Summer Jelled Coleslaw Salad

1 small box lemon Jello
1 cup boiling water
½ cup real mayonnaise
¼ teaspoon salt
¼ teaspoon pepper
2 cups grated cabbage
½ cup grated carrots
1 small onion, chopped fine
½ cup celery, sliced thin
Cucumbers, 1 large, sliced thin, peeled
Paprika

Dissolve Jello and salt in boiling water and cool for 20 minutes. Slowly add mayonnaise, about 2 spoonfuls at a time, to the cooled Jello mixture and mix well. Add all other ingredients except the cucumbers and paprika. Place Jello and cabbage mixture in an oblong pan. Place cucumber slices on top of salad, sprinkle with paprika. Cover tightly and chill in refrigerator overnight or until firm.

Summer Salad

Chop until fine:
5 medium-sized, peeled fresh tomatoes
2 medium-sized, peeled onions
2 tablespoons parsley heads
3 peeled cucumbers
1 cup sliced celery
1 clove garlic (optional)

Place the chopped vegetables in a serving bowl. Mix and pour over vegetables:

½ cup honey
Dash of Tabasco sauce
¼ cup wine vinegar
½ teaspoon salt
1 tablespoon brandy

Toss vegetables to marinate and chill at least 2 hours before serving. Serve in little bowls. Garnish with a half of stuffed olive.

Note: More Tabasco and vinegar may be added to suit individual taste.

Summer Fruit Tray

1 cup sour cream
3 tablespoons firmly packed brown sugar
2 tablespoons rum
½ teaspoon cardamom
1 medium-sized pineapple
1 papaya
4 medium-sized bananas
2 tablespoons fresh lime juice

Stir together the sour cream, brown sugar, rum and cardamom. Cover and chill in refrigerator overnight.

About 2 hours before serving, cut pineapple in half through the crown. With a grapefruit knife, cut pineapple into chunks, discarding the core. Save the shells. Pile the cut pineapple into 1 shell half. Peel and seed papaya, cut into lengthwise strips. Peel and cut bananas into 1 inch slanting slices, coat all sides with lime juice, drain briefly, and arrange on tray with the pineapple and papaya. Cover and chill. Stir any remaining lime juice into the sour cream and rum mixture. Pour sauce lightly over fruit and serve.

Orange and Banana Salad with Wine

2 oranges, peeled and sliced
2 bananas, peeled and sliced
1 cup grapes, halved and seeded
3 fresh ripe pears
½ cup fresh orange juice
½ cup dry white wine

Core and peel pears, cut into bite-sized pieces. Cut orange slices into halves.

Toss all fruit together. Pour orange juice and wine over all. Toss lightly. Chill and serve.

Orange and Banana Salad with Cool Whip or Whipped Cream

2 oranges, peeled and cut into small chunks
2 bananas, peeled and sliced
1 cup whipped cream or 1 cup Cool Whip

Mix all together and serve.

24 Hour Sauerkraut Salad

2 cans drained sauerkraut
½ can chopped pimiento
2 onions, chopped
1 green bell pepper, chopped
3 cups sugar
1 cup oil
1 cup vinegar

Mix well and let set in refrigerator for 24 hours. Serve.

24 Hour Salad

2 eggs beaten
4 tablespoons sugar
4 tablespoons vinegar
2 tablespoons butter

Cook all together. Cool. This is the dressing.

1 cup white cherries
2 cups cubed pineapple
2 cups cut up marshmallows
2 oranges, cut into small pieces,
   or 1 can mandarin oranges
1 cup cream, whipped

Mix all the fruit together. When the dressing has cooled add the whipped cream to the dressing. Fold into the fruit. Cover and refrigerate for 24 hours, serve in a square or oblong dish. My mother has served this at many a holiday feast.

Salad Marinades

LEMON HERBED MARINADE

½ cup chopped onion
½ cup lemon juice
¼ cup salad oil
½ teaspoon salt
½ teaspoon pepper
½ teaspoon thyme
½ teaspoon marjoram
½ teaspoon rosemary

Combine onion, lemon, oil, salt, pepper, thyme, marjoram and rosemary. Mix well. Yields 1¼ cups.

BURGUNDY WINE MARINADE

¾ cup burgundy wine
3 tablespoons salad oil
2 tablespoons chopped green onion
2 teaspoons brown sugar
1 teaspoon salt
1 clove garlic, quartered

Combine wine, oil, green onion, brown sugar, salt and garlic. Shake well. Remove garlic before serving. Yields 1 cup.

MEXICAN-STYLE MARINADE

⅓ cup tomato juice
⅓ cup vinegar
⅓ cup salad oil
1 4-oz. can green chilies,
 chopped and drained
1 teaspoon sugar
1 teaspoon salt
½ teaspoon cumin

Combine tomato juice, oil, vinegar, chilies, sugar, salt, and cumin. Beat well. Yields 1¼ cups.

Note: 2 fresh chilies may be used.

Italian Garlic Mayonnaise

4 larges cloves garlic
2 large egg yolks
1 teaspoon dry mustard
¼ teaspoon salt
¼ teaspoon white pepper
1 cup olive oil
1½ tablespoon lemon juice

Have all ingredients at room temperature. Peel garlic. Combine garlic, egg yolks, mustard, salt and pepper in blender container. Cover and blend until smooth.

With blender running, remove cover and slowly pour in half the oil in a small steady stream. Stop the motor and scrape down the sides with a spatula. Cover and turn to medium speed, then uncover and add the lemon juice and remaining oil in a slow stream, stopping to scrape down sides as needed. Beat until sauce thickens. Chill. Very good with artichokes. Also good with crumbled Roquefort cheese added for a salad dressing.

Roquefort Dressing

Serves 5 to 6 people.

½ cup sour cream
½ cup real mayonnaise
½ cup crumbled Roquefort cheese
1 tablespoon onion, grated
4 dashes Tabasco sauce
4 dashes worcestershire sauce
Salt to taste, dash white pepper
Juice of ½ lemon or lime
(you may substitute a tablespoon of red wine vinegar for the juice of the lemon or lime)

Mix all together. Chill before serving. This is an excellent recipe and has won many compliments at our house. Not only is it good on salads, but wonderful as a dip for fresh vegetables. Even try it on your hamburger.

For those large amounts of salad dressing:

Oil & Vinegar

1 quart of Wesson oil
1½ quarts vinegar
1½ pints chili sauce
2 cups sugar
Garlic salt or 1 clove
garlic, chopped
Dash of Salad Supreme

Mix well.

Thousand Island Dressing

1 gallon mayonnaise
1½ pints chili sauce
Generous shake of worcestershire
sauce
Generous shake of Tabasco sauce
2 cups pickle relish

Roquefort Cheese Dressing

1 gallon mayonnaise
5 pounds sour cream
4 pounds French Roquefort cheese
20 dashes Worcestershire sauce
20 dashes Tabasco sauce
Juice of one lemon
1 large onion, grated

French Dressing

½ cup vinegar
1 can tomato soup
1 cup Mazola oil
1 tablespoon worcestershire sauce
½ cup sugar
½ cup grated onion
1 teaspoon paprika

Mix well.

Selecting Fresh Produce

It is always a good rule to choose the fresh and avoid the shriveled, wilted or decayed.

Experience is the best teacher in choosing quality but here are a few pointers on buying some of the fruits and vegetables.

Apples: Good color usually indicates full flavor. Learn the varieties you like best for cooking and eating out of hand by buying small amounts, especially if you plan to buy a large amount later. Remember that the same apple you buy in the fall will be tart and it may be mellow in the spring.

Asparagus: Stalks should be tender and firm, tips should be close and compact. Choose the stalks with very little white, they are more tender. You should use asparagus soon after purchase as it toughens rapidly.

Beans, Snap: Those with small white seeds inside the pockets are best. Avoid beans that the pods look dried.

Berries: Select plump, solid berries with good color. Avoid stained containers, indicating wet or leaky berries. Berries such as blackberries and raspberries with clinging caps may be underripe. Strawberries without caps may be overripe.

Broccoli, Brussels Sprouts and Cauliflower: Flower clusters on broccoli and cauliflower should be tight and close together. Brussels sprouts should be firm and compact. Smudgy, dirty spots may indicate insects.

Cabbage and Head Lettuce: Choose heads heavy for size. Avoid cabbage with worm holes or lettuce with discoloration or soft rot.

Cucumbers: Choose long, slender cucumbers for best quality. May be dark or medium green. Yellow ones are undesirable.

Melons: In cantaloupes, thick close netting on the rind indicates best quality. Cantaloupes are ripe when the stem scar is smooth and space between the netting is yellow or yellow green. They are best to eat when fully ripe with fruity odor.

Honeydews are ripe when rind has a creamy to yellowish color and velvety texture. Immature honeydews are whitish green in color.

Ripe watermelons have some yellow color on one side. If melons are white or pale green on one side, they are not ripe.

Onions: Size and color do not affect flavor or quality. Avoid onions with wet necks. The Bermuda and Spanish types are milder than the very hard, long-keeping white varieties.

Oranges, Grapefruit and Lemons: Choose those heavy for their size. Smoother, thinner skins usually indicate more juice. (I was once told these were the male ones.) Most skin markings do not affect quality. Oranges with a slight greenish tinge may be just as ripe as fully colored ones. Light or greenish-yellow lemons are more tart than deep yellow ones. Avoid citrus fruits showing withered, sunken or soft areas.

Peaches: Best to buy when firm, not bruised, and showing no green color. Will ripen if left at room temperature.

Peas and Lima Beans: Select pods that are well-filled but not bulging. Avoid dried, spotted, yellowed or flabby pods.

Pears: Some pears, especially winter varieties, are marketed when slightly underripe and need to be ripened at home — at room temperature. Pears are ripe and ready to eat when they are slightly soft at stem end.

Potatoes: If you plan to buy a large quantity of potatoes, buy a few first to see if they are the kind that you want. Early crop potatoes, marketed in the summer, tend to be less mealy when cooked than those that are harvested later. Also the early ones have soft skins. Avoid potatoes with wasteful deep eyes.

Root Vegetables: Should be smooth and firm. Very large carrots may have woody cores, oversized radishes may be woody or pithy. Oversized turnips, beets and parsnips may be woody. Fresh carrot tops usually mean fresh carrots, but condition of leaves on most other root vegetables does not indicate degree of freshness.

Sweet Potatoes: Puerto Rico and Nancy Hall varieties — with bronze to rosy skins are soft and sweet when cooked. Yellow to light-brown ones are firmer and less moist.

Helpful Household Hints

For those pans that are burned black and are hard to clean, put 2 tablespoons fo dishwasher soap in them and fill with hot water, let set for 2 to 3 hours and wipe clean.

After you chop garlic, wash your hands with vinegar or rub them with a half of a lemon.

To get those tough grease stains out, rub with a cup of Coca-Cola.

What to do with that overripe avocado? Treat yourself to one of the finest moments of your life. Mash the avocado in a bowl. Now head for the bathroom and lock the door, rub the mashed avocado all over your face and let it set for 10 minutes. Clean with warm water, and now you feel so fresh and good. What a treat!

When cooking pancakes on a hot grill, instead of using grease or butter, rub the grill with a cut raw potato; use again after each batch.

MEAT DISHES

Rice
Potatoes
Eggs
Fish

Cowboy Beans

2 lbs. pinto beans
2 lbs. ham hocks or salt pork
2 onions, chopped
4 tablespoons sugar
2 green chilies
1 can tomato paste

Wash beans and soak overnight with 1 teaspoon baking soda. Drain. Rinse, cover with cold water. Place in a Dutch oven and cover with water. Add remaining ingredients and simmer until tender. Sample while cooking. Add salt to taste. Add water if needed.

Mexican Pinto Beans

Silver City, New Mexico, smoke jumpers were the first people to introduce me to this great recipe. Their version was quite a lot larger, but almost the same.

3 cups dry pinto beans
2 onions, chopped
¼ cup salsa brava, hot
½ jar La Victoria salsa
jalapena relish (hot)
1 can tomato sauce
1 small can whole tomatoes
1 can enchilada sauce, mild
One jalapeno pepper, hot
1 pound of ground beef,
lightly browned in skillet
1 tablespoon chili pepper (optional)

Soak beans overnight in 1 teaspoon of soda and enough water to cover beans one inch. Next morning drain liquid off beans, rinse. Put beans in a large, heavy pan or Dutch oven. Add onions, salsa brava, salsa jalapena, tomato sauce, enchilada sauce, chili pepper, browned ground meat and enough salt to taste. Cover with one inch of water. One tablespoon of chili powder may be added. Bring to a boil and turn to simmer and cook until beans are tender.

Beer Batter for Fish & Chips

6 ounces plain flour
½ level teaspoon salt
2 eggs, separated
4 ounces beer
2 tablespoons melted butter

Sift flour and salt into a bowl and make a well in the center.

Beat egg yolks lightly with beer and pour into well. With a wooden spoon gradually stir in the flour from the sides of the well until smooth.

Stir in the melted butter and allow batter to sit for about an hour.

When ready to use batter, whisk egg whites until stiff, but not dry, and fold in gently but thoroughly into batter.

Fish & Chips

1½ lbs. cod or halibut
(I use halibut because it seems to have more flavor)
Juice from two lemons
½ onion finely chopped
Salt and freshly ground black pepper
6 medium size potatoes
Oil for deep frying
Beer batter (see recipe above)
4 ounces sifted flour
1 level teaspoon paprika
Cayenne pepper, seasoned salt
2 lemons, cut into wedges

Cut fish into serving pieces, 2 or 3 per serving.

Place fish in a flat porcelain bowl and sprinkle with lemon juice, finely chopped onion and salt and freshly ground pepper, to taste. Allow fish to marinate in this mixture for 1 hour.

To make "chips," wash and peel the potatoes, cutting them into strips about ⅛ inch square and 3 inches long. Rinse in cold water and drain thoroughly.

Heat oil to 375°. Fill frying basket one-half to two-thirds full of potatoes and immerse it gently in the hot oil. Shake basket from time to time while frying to keep potatoes from sticking together. Continue to fry until potatoes are nearly tender. Drain well and spread on a pan lined with paper towels to absorb excess oil while you fry remaining potatoes.

Sift flour, paprika, seasoned salt and freshly ground black pepper, and cayenne pepper to taste, onto flat dish. Dust the fish thoroughly in the seasoned flour.

Dip the fish piece by piece into the batter and deep fry in same oil, making sure the heat is 375°, until golden brown and crisp. Place fish in a pan lined with paper towels and keep warm.

Bring oil to 375° again and refry potatoes until golden brown. Drain.

Serve fish and chips together in a heated serving dish. Garnish with lemon wedges.

Pat's Broccoli Casserole

1½ bunches broccoli, cooked
until almost done
Dash of salt
1½ cups fresh mushroom buds
1 small red onion, sliced and separated
3 tablespoons melted butter
1 can cream of chicken soup
1 cup grated Parmesan cheese
½ cup milk
Crushed corn flakes
(about ¼ cup)
½ cup shredded Cheddar cheese

Cook broccoli until tender but not completely done.

Butter an 8x8-inch baking dish. In microwave oven, cook mushroom buds, onions and butter for 4 minutes. Warm the can of cream of chicken soup, ½ cup milk and the Parmesan cheese in a pan until well blended. Place the drained broccoli, mushrooms, onions, cheese and chicken soup mixture in baking dish. Place the Cheddar cheese on top and sprinkle with the handful of crushed cornflakes. Bake in 325° F oven for 15 to 20 minutes.

Vienna Sausage & Noodles

½ cup each chopped onion and celery
1 cup grated carrot
¼ cup butter
3 tablespoons flour
1 teaspoon salt
1½ cups milk
½ cup real mayonnaise
½ teaspoon Worcestershire sauce
2 cups cooked noodles
2 5-oz. cans Vienna sausages in
beef stock, drained

Heat oven to 350° F. Cook onion, celery, carrot in butter for 5 minutes. Stir in flour, salt, milk; cook stirring constantly until thickened. Stir in mayonnaise, Worcestershire sauce, noodles, and sausages. Place in 1½ quart casserole. Bake uncovered at 350° for 25 minutes.

Harvard Beets or Carrots

⅓ cup sugar
4 tablespoons vinegar or lemon juice
2 tablespoons salad oil
12 small beets or canned beets or
2 bunches small carrots
½ tablespoon cornstarch
¼ cup water

Mix sugar and cornstarch. Add vinegar, oil and water. Boil 5 minutes, stirring constantly. Add beets (or carrots), cover and simmer 15 minutes.

Fluffy Eggs

For that special Sunday morning breakfast when you want to impress your sweetheart this is one nice way to present your eggs.

Separate eggs, saving the yolks in one half of the shell. The shell may be supported in a cup or dish.

Add salt to the whites, a scant ⅛ teaspoon per white. Beat the whites until stiff and glossy. Pile the whites on rounds of toast or squares of toast placed on a cookie sheet. Make a hollow in each with the back of a spoon. Drop an egg yolk into each hollow. Bake in a hot oven 400° F until whites are lightly browned, 8 to 10 minutes. Serve at once.

Oriental Beef Steak Strips

2 lbs. beef round steak or rib eye steak, cut in 1 inch strips
2 tablespoons cooking fat
Water
⅓ cup soy sauce
2 teaspoons sugar
¼ teaspoon pepper, coarsely ground
1 clove garlic, chopped fine
3 carrots, sliced lengthwise in thin strips
2 green peppers, bell type, cut into 1 inch pieces
8 green onions, cut in 1½ inch pieces
½ lb. mushrooms, halved
1 8-oz. can water chestnuts, halved
2 tablespoons cornstarch
¼ cup water
Cooked rice

Cut steak into strips ⅛-inch thick and 3 to 4 inches long. Brown strips in cooking fat. Pour off drippings, measure and add water to make 1 cup. Combine with soy sauce, sugar, pepper and garlic and add to meat. Cover and cook slowly for 45 minutes. Using vegetable parer, cut carrots lengthwise into strips and cut strips in half. Add carrots and peppers, onions, mushrooms and water chestnuts to meat, cover and continue cooking 15 minutes. Combine cornstarch and water, add to thicken cooking liquid for gravy. Serve with cooked rice. Top with additional chopped green onion tops. Makes 6 to 8 servings.

Beef Cooked with Beer

2 tablespoons butter
1 medium onion, chopped
2 lbs. round steak or any other steak of your choice
1 teaspoon salt
Pepper to taste
2 tablespoons rendered fat or Crisco
2 tablespoons flour
1 10-ounce glass of beer, light, not dark
1 tablespoon vinegar
Pinch of thyme
3 cups beef stock or consomme
1 tablespoon sugar
Sprig of parsley
1 large celery rib, whole
2 bay leaves
1 clove garlic, minced

In a small pan, brown the onions and garlic to a light golden color. Set aside. Trim all fat from meat. Flatten a little. Cut into 12 pieces. Season each piece with salt and pepper. Put Crisco or fat into a medium size frying pan. When very hot brown meat a few pieces at a time. As meat is done, place in an oven-ware casserole or Dutch oven. Add onions so that meat and onions are layered. In same frying pan add the flour and cook until it is well browned. Lower heat and add beer, vinegar, beef broth and sugar. Boil slowly, stirring until smooth. Add spices, parsley and celery to meat and onions. Pour sauce over all. Bring to a boil on top of stove. Put in a hot oven (425°) and cook 1½ to 2 hours until meat is tender. Discard celery, parsley, and bay leaves. Serve sauce as is or strain it. Serve over beef.

The No-Bean Beef Chili

2 tablespoons Crisco
3 medium onions, finely chopped
10 to 12 cloves garlic, finely chopped
3 lbs. beef chuck roast, cut into ¾-inch cubes
1 28-oz. can peeled tomatoes or 1 quart of home canned tomatoes
1½ tablespoons cumin powder (comino)
2 teaspoons marjoram
1 tablespoon Lawry's Seasoned Salt
1 teaspoon salt
1 tablespoon paprika
1 tablespoon red cayenne pepper
3 tablespoons of pulp from red dried Santa Cruz peppers (see note)
5 tablespoons (more or less) Santa Cruz chili pepper (powder)

In the Crisco saute the onions and garlic, then add the meat. Sear the meat until brown. Add tomatoes, including all liquid. Simmer for 2 hours, or until meat is tender. Then add all other ingredients and simmer for another 1 or 2 hours. This chili is and should be really thick.

We at our house like to serve this chili over rice. It is wonderful served with beans and rice. Any favorite bean recipe. I use the pinto beans, cooked with an onion and some chili powder.

A hot slice of homemade sourdough bread, a slice of Cheddar cheese, and a bowl of this chili (with or without beans and rice) will be a meal no one will ever forget. Served along with a cold glass of beer.

Note: Red dried Santa Cruz chili peppers can be found in most markets. Boil them in a pot of boiling water until soft. Put onto a piece of plastic paper and split and scrape out meat from the skins. Wear rubber gloves to keep hot pepper from burning your fingers. The paste from Santa Cruz chili peppers can also be purchased from your grocery store.

Chinese Dish

For 50 people.

10 lbs. lean pork or chicken
¾ cup fat or oil
1½ gallons of bean sprouts or cubed pineapple
¾ gallon celery, chopped in 1 inch pieces
1¼ quarts of onions, diced
⅛ cup salt
1 teaspoon pepper
½ cup sugar
1½ cups soy sauce
2⅛ cups cornstarch
1 cup cold water

Brown meat, add liquid from bean sprouts or pineapple juice and simmer 30 minutes. Add celery, onions, bean sprouts, salt, pepper and sugar. If pineapple is used add at the last 10 minutes. Add soy sauce last and cornstarch mixed with 1 cup cold water to meat mixture and simmer until slightly thickened. Serve over Chinese noodles or rice. You may use blanched almonds as a garnish if desired.

Hungarian Goulash

For 80 to 90 people.

25 lbs. boneless beef shoulder
½ lb. shortening
2 lbs. onions, quartered
2 ounces paprika
Meat stock to cover
2 green peppers, chopped
1 pint celery, diced in 1-inch pieces
1 lb. carrots, quartered
1½ quarts tomatoes, whole
Salt as needed
1 teaspoon red pepper, or
3 tablespoons Santa Cruz
pepper pulp
¾ cup flour
8 pounds potatoes, quartered

Cut beef into 1½ inch cubes. Mix with ¾ cup flour. Brown in a large roasting pan in the ¼ cup of the shortening. Saute the onions in the other ¼ cup of shortening. Sprinkle the paprika over the onions. Add to meat. Cover with stock. Cook 1 hour over medium heat. Stir in the celery and carrots, add peppers, and tomatoes. Add the hot pepper or pepper pulp. Cook for another 1 hour, or until the meat is tender. Add the potatoes. Cook for ½ hour longer. Serve with green peas or cole slaw and Hot Sourdough Biscuits are a must with this.

Grits and Greens

1 cup grits
1 teaspoon salt
4 cups boiling water
1 pkg. frozen spinach, thawed, well drained
2 cups shredded natural Swiss cheese
1½ cups diced ham
2 eggs, beaten
1 tablespoon prepared mustard
¼ cup grated Parmesan cheese

Prepare grits in salted water as directed on package. Add spinach, Swiss cheese and ham. Continue to cook 2 to 3 minutes, stirring frequently until the Swiss cheese is melted. Remove from heat; stir in eggs and mustard. Pour into a 2-quart casserole. Top with Parmesan cheese. Bake in preheated oven (350°) 30 minutes or until golden brown.

Joe's Special from San Francisco

(My Version)

1 lb. ground beef
½ cup chopped onions
1 4-oz. can sliced mushrooms or 1 cup sliced fresh mushrooms
1 pkg. (10 oz.) frozen chopped spinach, thawed or fresh
Garlic to taste (1 clove finely chopped)
¼ to ½ teaspoon oregano, basil or marjoram
4 eggs well beaten

Brown the beef until crumbly, drain off fat, add mushrooms, onions, spinach and spices.

Cook and stir for about 4 minutes or until onions are tender and the spinach is cooked.

Add the eggs and cook until the eggs are set.

Serve hot with a Sourdough Biscuit.

Jalapeno, Onion, Cheddar Cheese Potatoes

1 large fresh hot Jalapeno pepper, chopped fine
3 large potatoes, peeled, quartered and sliced thin
⅓ cup onion, chopped fine
1 cup milk, more if needed
½ cup cracker crumbs
2 tablespoons butter, softened
5 slices sharp Cheddar cheese, ⅓ inch thick
Salt and pepper to taste

One oblong baking dish 8x4½ x 4½ or one square baking dish 8x8 inches. Rub softened butter on inside of dish. Start a layer with ½ of the potatoes, then all of the onions. Sprinkle ½ of the cracker crumbs, and all of the pepper pieces on top of the onions. Cover with 2 slices of the cheese. Top with the rest of the potatoes and cracker crumbs. Pour the milk on top, sprinkle with salt and pepper. Be sure that all of the potatoes are covered with the milk. If not add more milk. Cook uncovered for 1 hour at 375° or until the potatoes are done but not mushy. 10 minutes before done top with the remaining 3 pieces of Cheddar cheese and leave until cheese is melted. Serve hot. Serves 4 people.

Delmonico Potatoes

4 cups potatoes (sliced and cooked until almost done)
1 can cream of mushroom soup
½ cup milk or cream
¼ cup onion
½ cup thinly sliced fresh mushrooms
4 crackers, smashed
½ cup grated Cheddar cheese
Salt and pepper to taste
Dash of butter

Cook the 4 cups of sliced potatoes until almost done. Drain. Mix the can of mushroom soup with the milk or cream.

Grease an 8x8 Pyrex baking dish with the butter. Put in layers of potatoes, onions, fresh mushrooms, crackers, salt and pepper, small amount of the cheese. Pour over this ½ of the cream of mushroom soup mixture. Add the rest of the potatoes, crackers, fresh mushrooms, onions and the rest of the soup mixture. Sprinkle the remainder of the Cheddar cheese on top. Sprinkle a scant of paprika on top.

Bake 45 minutes in oven at 350° F.

Heaven and Earth Potatoes

4 large potatoes, peeled and cut into pieces
4 tart apples, peeled, cored and cut into pieces
Salt to taste
Sugar to taste
⅛ teaspoon ground nutmeg
4 tablespoons butter, room temperature

Cook the potatoes in enough water to cover for about 10 minutes or until they are about ¾ done.

Drain off half the water. Add the apples, mix and cook until they are tender. Drain.

Mash the mixture and season with the salt, sugar, pepper, and nutmeg. Top with butter when serving.

Patio Potatoes

4 medium potatoes
3 tablespoons butter
3 tablespoons flour
2 cups milk
2 cups Cheddar cheese, grated
1 4-oz. can green chilies (hot), chopped
1 teaspoon salt
2 cloves garlic, crushed
½ cup buttered bread crumbs

Boil potatoes, peel, slice thinly and layer in a 1½ quart baking dish. Melt butter, stir in flour and gradually add milk, cook until mixture thickens slightly. Add cheese, chilies, salt and garlic. Pour mixture over potatoes and stir sauce through so all potatoes are coated. Top with bread crumbs. Bake at 350° for 25 minutes or until bread crumbs are browned.

Salmon Cakes

3 cups soft day-old sourdough
bread crumbs
3 eggs, slightly beaten
Dash of tabasco sauce (2 or 3 drops)
½ teaspoon salt
Ground pepper to taste
½ cup finely chopped onions
1 garlic clove, minced or pulverized
with garlic press
1 teaspoon seasoned salt
2 cups boned canned salmon
Dash of thyme
3 tablespoons butter
3 tablespoons vegetable oil

Combine 2 cups of bread crumbs (make bread crumbs in your blender), add 3 eggs, Tabasco sauce, salt, pepper. Add onions, garlic and thyme. Mix well. Add salmon. Mix and pat into 10 equal portions. Pat into shapes of 3-inch rounds and approximately ½ inch thick.

Spread remaining 1 cup crumbs on plate. Mix with the seasoned salt. Turn patties into the seasoned bread crumbs to coat lightly on both sides.

Preheat oven to low setting at 200°.

In a heavy skillet melt the butter and oil over moderate heat.

When hot add 3 or 4 patties at a time. Fry them 4 to 5 minutes on each side or until golden brown. Be sure to regulate heat so they brown evenly and do not burn.

As cakes are browned on both sides, transfer them to a shallow baking dish and set in warm oven, while you fry the rest. Arrange on heated platter and serve with lemon wedges.

Hot Spanish Rice

1 spoonful lard (tablespoon)
1 onion (cebollo)
1 cup rice (arroz)
½ cup peas (optional)
1 large pickled carrot
1 clove garlic (ajo)
3 cups beef broth
Salt to taste
One large Jalapeno pepper

Cook rice in broth along with the chopped onion, garlic, carrot, peas, lard and chopped jalapeno pepper. Bring to boil. Turn heat to low and simmer for 20 minutes. This is wonderful with any Spanish dish.

Pork Fried Rice

1 lb. of pork roast, which has been cooked
1 teaspoon ground ginger
3 tablespoon soy sauce
¼ cup honey
¼ cup dry sherry
3 tablespoons butter
2 cups long grain rice, cooked
½ teaspoon salt
8 green onions, chopped
2 eggs

In a large heavy skillet, brown the pork, which has been cut into long thin strips, in the butter. Add the ginger and soy sauce. Toss until the pork is well coated, stirring constantly. Add honey and continue to cook, stirring until all pieces are well glazed. Stir in sherry and put aside.

In a saucepan melt 2 tablespoons butter and add the rice. Swirl the pan until all the rice is coated, cook over low or medium heat until the rice is slightly browned. Transfer rice to the skillet with the pork. Add the onions and simmer for a few more minutes, stirring constantly. Move the rice and pork mixture to the outside of the skillet, leaving a ring in the center about 5 inches. Melt 1 tablespoon of butter in the center of ring, break the eggs into the center of cleared area. With a spatula, scramble the eggs and let them cook. Again using the spatula, cut the eggs into thin pieces and mix together with the rice and pork. More soy sauce may be added to taste.

To Cook A Large Amount Of Rice

1 lb. of rice
1 quart plus 1 cup of water
Salt to taste
2 tablespoons butter

Sweet & Sour Fruited Ham Served with White Rice

1 1-lb. 4-oz. can pineapple chunks
½ cup sugar
3 tablespoons cornstarch
1 teaspoon ginger or fresh ground
ginger root
½ teaspoon salt
½ cup juice from pineapple chunks
⅓ cup vinegar
1 tablespoon soy sauce
2 cups diced fully cooked ham
1 cup seedless green grapes
12 maraschino cherries, halved
6 servings of hot rice (steamed)
Toasted slivered almonds for garnish
2 cups water

Drain pineapple chunks (save syrup). Combine sugar, cornstarch, ginger and salt in saucepan; mix well. Combine reserved pineapple syrup, vinegar and soy sauce, add the 2 cups water. Stir into the sugar mixture. Cook stirring constantly, until thickened and clear. Add pineapple chunks, ham, grapes and cherries, mix carefully. Heat. Serve over rice, sprinkle with almonds.

Baked Lamb Stew

3 lbs. boneless stewing lamb,
cut into 1 inch pieces
6 tablespoons cooking oil
½ teaspoon salt
½ teaspoon ground pepper
½ cup flour
2½ cups beef broth
¼ cup dry sherry or white wine
2 cloves garlic, crushed
24 small onions or 1 large onion, diced
2 thinly sliced carrots
6 medium mushrooms, sliced
½ teaspoon dried marjoram
½ teaspoon thyme
2½ tablespoons lemon juice
3 tablespoons parsley

Dry lamb with paper towels. Brown well in heated oil in frying pan, place meat into an ovenproof casserole. Combine salt, pepper and flour. Sprinkle over lamb, mix well. Add heated broth, sherry, garlic. Cover and bake at 350° F for 1 hour. Add onions, carrots, mushrooms and herbs, cook half hour more. Let stand 10 minutes uncovered; skim off fat. Add lemon juice and parsley, stir gently. Serve at once with rice.

Ground Lamb Chili

2 cups dry pinto beans

Sort and wash the beans. Soak overnight with ½ teaspoon baking soda and enough water to cover them 2 inches.

Next morning drain off water, and cover with 2 inches of fresh water.

Now add 1 large can of tomatoes, or 1 pt. of home canned tomatoes, ½ teaspoon salt, 1 jalapeno pepper (fresh whole one), ½ of a large onion chopped, and 1 teaspoon of red hot chili peppers, mashed. Cover and cook until beans are tender.

Meanwhile cook in a large skillet 1½ lbs. of ground lamb, ½ large onion, chopped; salt and coarsely ground black pepper; 1 large clove of garlic, chopped. Brown until onions are clear and lamb is still pink in center. Stir in 1 cup tomato soup, 3 tablespoons ground chili powder. Now add meat mixture to beans and simmer for 20 minutes. Serve with shredded sharp Cheddar cheese, chopped fresh jalapenos, and a slice of hot sourdough bread. Also wonderful served with jalapeno cornbread.

Lamb Stew

(Robbie's)

2 oz. butter
2 medium onions, finely chopped
3 lbs. lamb shoulder (after all
  the fat has been trimmed),
  cut into cubes
Salt and pepper (I prefer the
  coarsely ground pepper)
1 teaspoon of seasoned salt
1 8-oz. can of tomato sauce
3 cups of chicken broth
¾ teaspoon thyme
4 garlic cloves (may be added or less
  according to taste), chopped
1 small bay leaf
3 stalks of celery
3 medium carrots
16 small white onions
½ to 1 lb. mushrooms
  (small caps only)

Melt butter in a large stew-pot. Saute the onions, finely chopped, until they are golden. Add the trimmed, cubed lamb. Sprinkle with the salt and pepper and seasoned salt, and brown well on all sides. Add the tomato sauce, chicken broth, thyme, garlic cloves and bay leaf. When the liquid is boiling, cover the pot and simmer for 1 hour, stirring occasionally. Cut the carrots and celery in medium sized pieces and add to the stew pot. If you are using fresh small onions add them at this time. Cover and simmer for another hour. Clean the mushroom caps and add to the stew. Cover and cook for another half hour until meat is done and tender. Let stew stand for a few minutes to let the fat rise to the top. Remove as much fat as possible. Turn into serving dish and serve with hot sourdough biscuits.

Leg of Lamb with Wine and Mustard Sauce

1 boned and rolled leg of lamb,
about 5 lbs.
¼ cup hot or sweet German mustard
4 slices bacon
¼ cup butter
½ cup chopped onion
1 carrot, sliced
1 clove garlic, minced
2 celery sticks, sliced
1 cup dry white wine
2 tablespoons cold water
1½ tablespoons cornstarch

Spread lamb with mustard. Refrigerate and let set overnight. Melt butter in the roasting pan; brown lamb on all sides. Place bacon on top of lamb and add remaining ingredients to pan. Roast at 350° for 2½ to 3 hours, or until done, basting with juices from pan. Place meat on platter. Strain vegetables from pan juices. Save juices. Return juices to pan. Skim off fat. Blend water and cornstarch together; stir into liquid in the pan. Place over medium heat until liquid thickens. Serve with lamb.

Lamb Stuffed, Sweet Red Peppers

6 large, firm, sweet red peppers
1½ lbs. ground lamb
1½ cup mushrooms, chopped
3 ripe tomatoes, chopped
½ cup onions, chopped
1 tablespoon butter
1 teaspoon salt
½ teaspoon seasoned salt
½ teaspoon marjoram
¼ teaspoon fresh ground pepper
1 large clove garlic, chopped very fine
1 cup dry bread crumbs, or prepared
poultry stuffing

Wash peppers, core, remove seeds and drain well. Save any red parts from tops, chop into small pieces. In a large skillet, brown the lamb in the butter. Add the onions, mushrooms and pepper tops, saute until onions are golden brown. Add remaining ingredients and simmer for 30 minutes. Spoon meat into and onto peppers. Place peppers into a shallow baking dish. Bake at 30 minutes at 350° F. Serves 3 to 6 people. This dish may be made up ahead of time to the point of putting the dish into the oven. Cook 30 minutes before serving. Serve at once.

Italian Sausage with Cabbage

2 lbs. link Italian sausage
2 cups dry red wine
1 clove garlic, minced
½ cup finely chopped onion
2 tablespoons finely chopped salt pork
1 16-oz. can stewed tomatoes, cut up
1 cup water
1 medium head cabbage,
coarsely chopped
Salt and pepper, coarsely ground

Using fork, prick sausage casing several times. Cook sausage in hot, boiling water for 20 minutes. Drain and cool. Cut sausage into 3-inch pieces. Place sausage in large mixing bowl. Add wine and minced garlic. Set sausage aside to marinate for 30 minutes. Drain sausage, reserving marinade. In large saucepan or Dutch oven cook sausage, onion and salt pork until meat is browned and onion is tender. Add the reserved wine marinade. Cover and simmer 20 minutes. Stir in undrained tomatoes, water and cabbage. Cover and simmer 20 minutes more, stirring occasionally. Season to taste with salt and pepper. Ladle into individual soup bowls to serve. Serve with sourdough bread or sourdough hard rolls. Makes 8 to 10 servings.

Round Steak Stroganoff

1½ to 2 lbs. of top round steak
½ cup flour
1 teaspoon salt
½ teaspoon pepper
1 teaspoon paprika
⅓ cup butter or margarine
1 cup diced onion
4 garlic cloves, cut fine
1 10½-oz. can beef consomme
Pinch of dry mustard
2 tablespoons chili sauce
1 lb. mushrooms, sliced
¼ cup sherry
1 pint sour cream

Cut meat into 1 inch thin strips. Combine flour, salt, pepper and paprika in paper bag. Shake meat strips in bag till well coated. Heat butter in Dutch oven or heavy pan, add meat strips and brown well, turning often. Add onions, garlic, cook till onions are golden, stirring frequently. Add consomme, mustard, chili sauce and stir well. Add mushrooms, sherry, cover and simmer till meat is tender, about 20 to 30 minutes. Stir in sour cream and heat gently. DO NOT BOIL. 6 to 8 servings. Serve over buttered noodles or rice.

Veal & White Wine Stroganoff

3 lbs. thinly sliced veal
¼ cup flour
1 teaspoon salt
½ teaspoon seasoned salt
¼ teaspoon fresh ground pepper
¼ teaspoon marjoram
¼ cup cooking oil
1 cup beef broth
1 tablespoon catsup or tomato sauce
1 teaspoon dry mustard
1 teaspoon Worcestershire sauce
1 cup dry white wine (I use
  Chardonnay by Robert Mondavi)
¼ lb. mushrooms, sliced
2 tablespoons finely chopped onions
1 tablespoon flour
¼ cup cold water
1 cup sour cream
Chopped parsley for garnish

Cut veal into strips 2 inches long and 1 inch wide. Combine flour with salts, pepper and marjoram. Sprinkle over meat, toss lightly to coat on all sides. Brown in oil in skillet. Stir in catsup, mustard and Worcestershire sauce. Simmer for 30 minutes. Stir in wine and mushrooms; continue to cook uncovered, for 15 minutes or until meat is tender. Combine flour with water to make a paste. Carefully stir into meat and stir for 5 minutes. Remove from heat. Stir in the sour cream. Sprinkle with parsley. Serve at once with noodles or rice. Goes nice with a summer salad.

Spaghetti, Italian Style

2 lbs. ground sirloin tip (your butcher will grind you a small tip roast)
1 cup chopped purple onion
2 cloves garlic, minced
2 large celery sticks, finely chopped
5 oz. of fresh mushrooms, trimmed and sliced (2 cups)
1 8-oz. can of Del Monte tomato sauce, plus enough water to rinse out can
1 qt. of home canned tomatoes or a large can of tomatoes, plus liquid
⅛ teaspoon cracked pepper
⅛ teaspoon Lawry's seasoned salt
½ teaspoon salt
⅛ teaspoon marjoram
⅛ teaspoon rosemary leaves (crushed)
⅛ teaspoon oregano

In a large Dutch oven or electric skillet, put the ground sirloin tip, onions, garlic and celery. Add seasoned salt, salt and pepper. Brown, stirring often, on medium heat until meat has browned and onions are clear in color. Add tomatoes, tomato sauce and mushrooms. Stir to mix well. Add spices. Mix. Cover and let simmer on low heat for 1 hour. Keep hot. Makes 8 cups of sauce. Serve over spaghetti.

Spaghetti: Cook 10 oz. of spaghetti in a pot of boiling water with a tablespoon of butter and a teaspoon salt. Cook for approximately 14 minutes. Drain in a wire basket or strainer. Rinse with real hot water. Serve at once with sauce. Serve with fresh grated Parmesan cheese. Good with hot sourdough garlic toast and your favorite tossed green salad.

Calories: 1 cup cooked spaghetti = 155 calories
1 cup cooked sauce = 200 calories
Parmesan cheese = 25 calories per tablespoon

Slow Cook Stew

1 lb. carrots, peeled and cut into cubes
½ lb. small white onions, peeled
2 lbs. potatoes, peeled and halved
2 lbs. boneless beef stew meat, cubed
2 sprigs parsley
2 cloves garlic, sliced
½ teaspoon tarragon leaves
½ teaspoon cracked black pepper
1 teaspoon salt
2 bay leaves
½ cup quick-cooking tapioca
(or 2 tablespoons flour)
1 1-lb. can tomatoes
1 cup water

Place carrots, onions, potatoes, stew meat, parsley and garlic in electric slow cooker in order given.

Mix tarragon, pepper, salt, bay leaves and tapioca or flour; sprinkle over stew ingredients. Pour tomatoes and water over all. Cover and turn heat to low and cook 5 to 7 hours or until meat is tender. Mushrooms may be added 1 hour before serving. Very good served with hot sourdough biscuits or French bread.

The Best Meatloaves Ever

3 eggs
¾ cup heavy cream
¾ cup beef broth
¾ cup sourdough French bread
crumbs
¾ cup finely chopped onion
3 cloves garlic, minced
3 tablespoons Worcestershire sauce
1½ teaspoons salt
1 teaspoon seasoned salt
½ teaspoon fresh ground pepper
1½ lbs. ground beef
1½ lbs. ground pork
1½ lbs. ground veal

Combine eggs, heavy cream and broth. Add remaining ingredients, mixing in ground meats lightly. Divide mixture into 3 parts, each of which will serve six. Bake in preheated oven 350° F, for 1 hour and 10 minutes to 1 hour and 20 minutes. Part of or all unbaked meat loaves may be frozen for later use.

This is good served with a sweet and sour sauce.

Saute ¼ cup chopped green peppers in 1 tablespoon vegetable oil until tender. Add 1 minced garlic clove. Add ½ cup each sugar and cider vinegar, ¼ cup drained canned pineapple tidbits, 2 tablespoons each chopped pimiento and soy sauce.

Dissolve 1½ tablespoons cornstarch in ½ cup cold water. Gradually add to sauce. Heat, stirring constantly, until thickened. Pour over cooked meatloaf and serve.

Prime Rib Roast

Set oven to 425° F.

Have your butcher cut you a 4-rib prime roast. Have him cut the ribs loose and tie in place.

Put the roast into a large roasting pan with the fat side up. Poke slashes into the meat with a small paring knife. Slice 3 cloves of garlic. Add these slices into the holes made with the knife, throughout the meat. To the pan add: 2 sliced carrots, one large quartered onion and one large stick of celery. Top the meat with 1 teaspoon coarse ground pepper, 1 teaspoon seasoned salt, 6 shakes of Worcestershire sauce and ¼ cup Pinot Noir Red Wine. Set into hot oven 425° F. and cook for 2 to 2½ hours. Baste with ¼ cup of wine again after the meat has been in the oven for 1 hour. Meat will be rare in the middle and well on the outside. Since Prime Rib has little taste or flavor, the garlic adds to the taste and the juices are still in the meat.

Before serving, remove the meat to a large platter. Take off the string. Let set for a few minutes. Meanwhile, scoop the carrots, onions, and celery from bottom of pan and discard. Add two tablespoons flour and set onto burner on top of stove. Mix until all flour has been absorbed. Add enough water to make a smooth gravy. Simmer for 5 minutes on low heat. Serve on the side of the meat or with mashed or baked potatoes.

Golden Fried Oysters

1 pt. fresh oysters
2 eggs, well beaten
2 tablespoons milk
1 teaspoon seasoned salt (Lawry's)
⅛ teaspoon fresh ground pepper
1 cup fine cracker crumbs

Drain oysters. Combine eggs, milk, and seasonings. Dip oysters in egg mixture and roll them in the cracker crumbs. Repeat process to form double breading. Let set half hour before frying.

Deep Fat Fried: Fry in oil, hot but not smoking (375°) until golden brown. Total frying time is 2 to 3 minutes. Drain on absorbent paper.

Pan Fried: Fry in ¼ inch of oil, hot but not smoking, until bottom side is golden brown, then turn and fry other side until golden brown. Makes 4 servings.

Mexican Shrimp in Hot Sauce Served with Steamed Rice

2 lbs. of large shrimp (blue) peeled and deveined. Save the peeled skins to boil for stock. (See note)
2 medium onions, chopped
2 stalks celery, chopped fine
3 tablespoons butter
1 bell pepper, chopped (green)
3 cloves garlic, minced
2 small ripe red tomatoes
½ cup chopped jalapeno peppers, fresh
1 bay leaf
1 teaspoon salt
1 teaspoon coarsely ground pepper
3 cups stock (See note)
2 tablespoons red Santa Cruz chili pepper pulp
Dash of Tabasco sauce

Heat in a large pan the butter, onions, celery and garlic, stirring often. Brown the onions until they are dark but not burned. Add the stock, peppers and tomatoes. Bring to a full boil. Add the spices and chili pulp. Cook until the sauce has cooked down and has thickened some. Cook over a low heat (about 1 hour). Add shrimp right before serving. Shrimp are done when they turn pink. Serve over steamed rice.

Note: To make a stock cook the shrimp skins in water, add onion, salt and pepper, a carrot and the tops of the celery sticks. If you have any other vegetables in the refrigerator, like broccoli, add to the stock. Cook until stock smells fresh and the vegetables are done. Strain. Use in recipe 3 cups.

Shrimp Cooked in Sherry Wine

½ stick butter
5 garlic cloves, crushed
1½ lb. shrimp, shelled and deveined
¼ cup lemon juice
¼ teaspoon freshly ground pepper
1 cup cooking sherry
2 tablespoons chopped parsley
2 tablespoons chopped chives
Salt to taste

Melt butter in skillet over medium heat. Add garlic, shrimp, lemon juice and pepper and salt. Cook, stirring until shrimp turns pink, about five minutes. Add wine, parsley and chives. Bring just to a boil. Serve immediately on a bed of rice. Garnish with lemon slices and parsley. Serves 4.

Barbecued Baby Back Ribs

2 full racks of baby back pork ribs
Seasoned salt to taste
Freshly ground pepper
2 cups Summer Barbecue sauce

Place ribs on a rack in a shallow open roasting pan. Sprinkle with the seasoned salt and freshly ground pepper. Bake in a preheated oven, 275°, for one hour or until done.

Meanwhile, start barbecue briquets. Let them burn down until they have a nice red ash.

Take ribs from oven, brush both sides with Summer Barbecue Sauce. Put onto grill and cover. Cook for 10 to 15 minutes on each side. Brush on sauce often. Cook until as tender as you desire them.

Heat any leftover sauce to serve on the side while eating.

See page 110 for Barbecue Sauce.

Mother's Barbecued Spareribs

(Tillie Larive)

4 lbs. beef ribs
1 teaspoon salt
2 bells garlic
1 bottle chili sauce
¼ cup fresh lemon juice
4 tablespoons butter
½ teaspoon dry mustard
2 tablespoons Worcestershire sauce
3 tablespoons brown sugar
3 teaspoons Tabasco sauce
  or red pepper
½ cup vinegar
½ cup water
Liquid smoke

Mix all the ingredients together except the liquid smoke. Baste the ribs with liquid smoke, cover with the sauce. Baste with more sauce as ribs are cooking. Bake until done. Approximately 1 hour in a slow oven 275° F.

Orange Flavored Yams

4 lbs.of yams
1 tablespoon butter
1 tablespoon honey
Juice from 2 oranges
1 teaspoon grated orange rind

Boil yams in water to cover, until tender. Drain, drop them into cold water to slip off skins. Mash yams and blend in remaining ingredients. Salt to taste. Put into buttered casserole. Bake at 325° F for 40 minutes or until slightly brown on top.

Turkey Glazed with Red Pinot Noir Wine and Cornbread Dressing

Cornbread (use any cornbread recipe, making it the day before and letting it dry out)
½ cup dark raisins
½ cup Cognac
1 turkey (about 16 pounds)
Butter
Salt
2 cups chopped onions
2 cloves garlic, minced
½ cup butter
1 lb. bulk pork sausage
1½ cups chopped tart apples
1 cup chopped celery
1 15-oz. can chestnuts, drained and chopped really fine
½ cup snipped parsley (optional)
1 tablespoon dried sage leaves
2 teaspoons dried marjoram
1 teaspoon thyme leaves
½ teaspoon cloves (ground)
2 teaspoons salt
1 teaspoon freshly ground pepper
4 eggs, beaten
Melted butter

Make cornbread. Cut into pieces or cubes; dry overnight.

Soak raisins in Cognac overnight.

Remove giblets, liver and neck from turkey, set aside or discard.

Rinse turkey, clean cavities, pat dry. Butter and salt cavities. Saute onions and garlic in ½ cup butter in a large skillet over medium heat until soft, about 5 minutes. Add sausage and celery; cook until sausage is brown, about 10 minutes. Stir in apples; cook until soft, about 10 minutes. Drain if too much fat in sausage. Combine reserved cornbread cubes, raisins and cognac mixture, sausage mixture and all remaining ingredients. Stir in eggs. Mix well. If more moisture is needed add a little milk or cream. Heat oven to 400° F. Fill cavities with stuffing; truss turkey. Insert meat thermometer so tip is in thickest part of inside thigh, away from bone. Place turkey, breast side up on rack in large roasting pan. Brush turkey with butter. Roast turkey at 400° until turkey starts to brown for the first hour. Baste with Pinot Noir frequently. Turn oven down after first hour to 375° and continue to bake until thermometer registers 175°, 4 to 4½ hours. Cover turkey loosely with a tent of aluminum foil when turkey starts to turn brown. Serve with favorite gravy.

Turkey or Chicken Rolls

Turkey or chicken, cooked and finely chopped (2 quarts or 2½ lbs.)
Instant mixed onions, 1 tablespoon (or 2 tablespoons finely chopped fresh onions)
1 tablespoon water (to soak dry onions if used)
2 cups celery, finely chopped
1 teaspoon salt
1 teaspoon pepper
2 cups shredded Cheddar cheese
1 cup mayonnaise
25 hamburger buns

Preheat oven to 350° F.

If dry onions are used soak them in the 1 tablespoon of water. Lightly mix turkey or chicken with onion, salt, pepper. Fold in the cheese. Add mayonnaise and mix gently. Spread mixture (¼ cup) on bottom half of each bun. Top with other half of bun. Place on a cookie sheet and heat for 15 minutes or until filling is hot and cheese is melted.

Calories: 310 per serving.

Hors d'Oeuvres & Snacks

Bourbon Balls

½ cup butter
1 lb. box confectioners' sugar
4½ teaspoons 100 proof bourbon
8 squares semi-sweet chocolate, broken into pieces
36 pecan halves

Beat butter in medium-size saucepan or bowl until light and fluffy. Gradually beat in the sugar. Slowly beat in the bourbon. Chill 1 hour or until mixture is stiff enough to shape. Roll into 1 inch balls. Arrange in a single layer on waxed paper-lined tray. Chill another hour.

Melt chocolate on top of double boiler over simmering, not boiling, water. Remove from heat; cool until a good dipping consistency. Dip bourbon balls with a 3-pronged fork halfway into chocolate. Return to waxed paper-lined tray. Place half pecan on top of each ball; when all the bourbon balls have been dipped, return tray to refrigerator. Chill until firm.

Choux Paste

¼ pint of cold water
½ lb. of flour (1¾ cups)
¼ lb. butter
6 eggs
Salt (small pinch)

Put water in a saucepan and add butter which has been divided into small pieces with a pinch of salt. Bring water to a boil on a quick fire and as soon as the mixture bubbles, remove from fire and add flour all at once and stir hard until paste is really smooth. Replace the saucepan to heat and stir until the paste no longer sticks or clings to the pan. Remove from heat and beat in the eggs one at a time, beating high to let plenty of air in. Roll the paste on a floured board — cut paste in either circles or squares. Fill one half of the paste with your favorite choice of meat mixture. Fold over the remaining half and crimp the edge securely. Place in a very hot oven if you wish a crisp paste and slower oven if you want it as a pie would be. Filling can be of your choice: meat, fruit, jam or anything that is interesting.

Clam Cream Cheese Dip

16-oz. cream cheese, mix until soft
2 cans of small clams, add to the
 cheese along with a small amount
 of the juice (about 1 tablespoon)
Mayonnaise to taste (about 1-2
 tablespoons)
1 tablespoon Worcestershire sauce
Salt to taste
Pepper to taste
2 teaspoons of minced onion
½ garlic clove, minced or
 dash of garlic salt to taste

Mix all ingredients together and refrigerate for a few hours before serving.

Cheese Balls

¼ cup butter
½ lb. grated Cheddar cheese
1 cup flour
1 pinch salt
1 pinch cayenne pepper

Mix above ingredients and form into small balls — half the size of walnuts. Bake in 350° oven for about 20 minutes. Serve hot.

Cheese Puffs

Combine ½ cup soft bread crumbs, ¼ cup grated Swiss cheese, 1 beaten egg yolk, 2 tablespoons chopped parsley, 1 teaspoon prepared mustard, ¼ teaspoon salt, pinch of cayenne. Beat egg white and fold into cheese mixture. Shape mixture into walnut-size balls. Roll in dry bread crumbs; place in a wire basket and fry in deep hot fat until puffs are just golden brown, about 1 minute.

Chicken Nut Filling

2 cups minced, cooked or canned chicken or turkey
½ cup minced celery
1 cup finely chopped pecans
⅓ cup mayonnaise or cooked salad dressing
½ teaspoon seasoned salt
¼ teaspoon pepper

Mix all together. Refrigerate. Makes 3½ cups filling. This is good in miniature cream puffs, as a salad on lettuce or as a sandwich spread. Also good stuffed in cherry tomatoes.

Small Cherry Tomatoes Stuffed with Avocado

1 cup tuna, drained
1 3-oz. pkg. cream cheese
1 ripe avocado, mashed
Juice from ½ of a lemon
1 teaspoon hot red pepper
½ teaspoon salt
½ teaspoon Tabasco sauce
½ teaspoon Worcestershire sauce
2 to 3 pints of cherry tomatoes

Drain tuna and crumble. Cream together the avocado and cream cheese. Add the seasonings and tuna to the cream cheese mixture. Wash and hollow out the centers of the tomatoes. Fill with the tuna, avocado mixture.

Alaska Pickled Crab Tails

(Rodney Littleton)

4 lbs. crab tails
3½ cups catsup
3½ cups vinegar
3 tablespoons salt
10-oz. bottle of Worcestershire sauce
5 teaspoons dry mustard
20 teaspoons sugar
10 dashes Tabasco sauce
10 dashes Johnney's salad elegance
(may be omitted)
2 medium onions, sliced
Bay leaf
Crushed garlic

Put crab tails on onions alternately in jars.
Mix all other ingredients together and add to crab tails.
These will keep in the refrigerator for up to a month.

Holiday Hot Crab Recipe

2 8-oz. packages cream cheese
⅓ cup mayonnaise
1½ teaspoons dry mustard
3 tablespoons white wine
4 teaspoons confectioners sugar
½ teaspoon salt
¼ teaspoon onion juice or 1 tablespoon
onion, ground fine
2 cans crabmeat, drained

Cream together cheese, mayonnaise and wine. Add rest of seasonings. Fold in crabmeat. Heat in double boiler or in oven at 325° for 20 minutes. Keep warm in chafing dish. Serve with firm crackers.

Pork and Crab Meat Balls

½ lb. fresh or canned crabmeat,
coarsely chopped
½ lb. ground pork
2 tablespoons chopped onion
½ cup chopped mushrooms
½ cup chopped water chestnuts
1 teaspoon salt
½ teaspoon pepper
1 teaspoon sugar
½ cup cornstarch
1 egg, beaten
1 tablespoon water
Fat for deep frying

Mix together the chopped crab meat, pork, chopped onion, chopped mushrooms, chopped chestnuts, salt, pepper and sugar. Shape into walnut size balls. Roll lightly in cornstarch; dip in the beaten egg mixed with the water.

Heat the fat to 360°, fry the balls for 15 minutes. Drain well.

Makes 35 balls. To serve, spear each ball with a toothpick.

Stuffed Dill Pickle

Cut off end of large dill pickle. Scoop out center. Drain thoroughly. Grind scooping with salami (enough to make a thick paste) plus 1 teaspoon onion (chopped). Add a package of Philadelphia cream cheese. Stuff dill pickle. Wrap and put in refrigerator until very cold. Slice just before serving. Continue doing this until several pickles are stuffed.

Another good cracker spread is the same as above using a 6-oz. package ground pepperoni, 2 large ground dill pickles, 3 tablespoons ground onion, and add a package of cream cheese and mix well. Chill and serve on Ritz crackers or tea sandwiches.

Polynesian Ginger Dip

1 cup mayonnaise, chilled
1 cup dairy sour cream
¼ cup finely chopped onion
¼ cup minced parsley
¼ cup finely chopped water chestnuts
1-2 tablespoons finely chopped candied or fresh ginger
1 tablespoon soy sauce
2 cloves garlic, minced
Dash salt or garlic powder

Combine mayonnaise and sour cream. Add remaining ingredients and mix well. Makes 2 cups.

Honey Snacks

⅓ cup butter, melted
⅓ cup packed brown sugar
¼ cup honey
3 cups 100% Natural Cereal

Combine butter, sugar and honey. Mix over low heat until smooth. Pour over cereal, mix well. Firmly pack into a foil lined 9-inch square baking pan. Bake in preheated very hot oven, 450° for 6-8 minutes. Mixture will be brown and bubbly. Cool. Invert pan on cutting board. Remove pan and foil. Cut into bite size pieces and serve.

Lobster Boats

½ lb. cooked, fresh or frozen lobster
24 fresh, large mushrooms, approximately 1½ inches in diameter
¼ can cream of mushroom soup
2 tablespoons of fine sourdough bread crumbs
3 tablespoons real mayonnaise
2 hard shakes of Worcestershire sauce
2 hard dashes of hot Tabasco sauce
Shake of salt
Shake of pepper
Grated sharp Cheddar cheese (about 1 cup)

Thaw frozen lobster meat. Drain. Remove any remaining shell or cartilage. Chop meat into fine pieces. Rinse mushrooms and remove the caps from the stems. Dry and set aside or onto a cookie sheet. Combine soup, crumbs, pepper and salt, mayonnaise, Worcestershire sauce, Tabasco sauce, and lobster. Stuff each mushroom cap with a tablespoon of the lobster mixture. Sprinkle with grated cheese. Place mushrooms on a greased cookie sheet and bake in a hot oven for 10 to 15 minutes at 450° F. Serve hot.

Pink Shrimp Dip

1 5-oz. can shrimp
1 cup creamy cottage cheese (large curd)
3 tablespoons chili sauce
½ teaspoon onion juice or very finely chopped onion
2 teaspoons lemon juice
¼ teaspoon Worcestershire sauce
⅓ cup milk

Finely chop shrimp, add the cottage cheese. Stir in the chili sauce, onion, lemon juice and Worcestershire sauce. Gradually beat in enough milk to give dipping consistency. Serve with potato chips or crackers.

Stuffed Mushrooms

12 large mushrooms (stems removed and stems chopped fine)
3 tablespoons butter
5 green onions, chopped fine
1 cup small shrimp, cooked
1 cup of day old sourdough bread crumbs
2 tablespoons sherry
Salt and pepper to taste
Dash of oregano
1 cup chopped spinach
½ cup shredded Cheddar cheese

Peel and wash mushrooms. Melt butter in a small saucepan. Add the chopped onions and mushroom parts, simmer for 2 minutes. Add bread crumbs and sherry, stir until well blended. Add salt and pepper, and oregano. Add shrimp. Stuff the mushroom caps with bread crumb mixture, top with the cooked chopped spinach and sprinkle with the Cheddar cheese. Bake for 10 to 15 minutes in a 350° oven. Serve hot.

Rum Balls

(Grandmother Lloyd's)

8 cups cake crumbs (assorted)
½ lb. pecans, chopped
1 cup rum
1 can 7-oz. flaked coconut

Combine cake crumbs, pecans and rum in a bowl. Mix and form into balls. Roll into coconut. Refrigerate until firm. Serve. Good for dessert at card games.

Marinated Veal

Have a butcher bone a breast of veal. Make the following marinade.

In 2 tablespoons of
butter, saute:
2 cloves garlic
1 shallot, chopped
1 bay leaf
1 sprig each of parsley and thyme
1 pinch of cumin seed

Add 4 cups of water and ¼ cup vinegar, bring the liquid to a boil and simmer for 30 minutes. Pour the marinade over the veal and let set for 12 hours.

Now dry the meat and cover it with bacon strips. Sprinkle the bacon with 1 onion, chopped, ½ cup chopped parsley, and salt and pepper to taste. Arrange lengthwise on top of bacon, 2 whole carrots and 2 whole hard-boiled eggs. Roll up the meat, secure with a string, wrap it in muslin and tie both ends. Bring the marinade to a boil and put in the meat, weighing it down with a lid or plate. Reduce the heat and simmer the veal for 2 hours, adding more liquid (hot water) as necessary to keep it covered. Chill the meat in the marinade and then remove the string and cloth. Slice it thinly and serve as hors d'oeuvres or with a green salad as a luncheon dish.

Football T.V. Treat

5 quarts popped corn
2 cups miniature marshmellows
1 cup whole roasted almonds
2 cups light brown sugar,
firmly packed brown sugar
½ cup light corn syrup
½ pound butter
¼ teaspoon cream of tarter
1 teaspoon salt
1 teaspoon soda

In a large roasting pan, combine popped corn, marshmellows, and almonds; set aside. In a 2½ quart saucepan, combine brown sugar, corn syrup, cream of tarter and salt. Bring to boil, stirring constantly over medium heat. Boil rapidly to a hard ball stage.

Remove from heat. Stir in baking soda quickly and thoroughly; pour immediately over popcorn mixture. Stir gently until well coated. Turn at once onto wax paper and spread out and allow to cool. Break apart. Store in an air tight container.

Mom's Popcorn Balls

2 cups white sugar
1 cup white corn syrup
2 teaspoons cream of tarter
1 tablespoon butter
½ teaspoon soda
6 quarts popped corn

Cook first 4 ingredients to a hard ball stage. Remove from fire. Add baking soda. Stir thoroughly. Pour over popped corn and form balls. Coloring and nut meats may be added if desired.

Mother's Taffy Apples

1 cup sugar
¾ cup dark corn syrup
2 tablespoons butter
1 teaspoon vanilla
1 cup light cream

Cook sugar, cream and butter on low heat. Cook to hard ball stage. Do not stir. Remove from fire, add vanilla. Keep warm over hot water. Dip apples into mixture, swivel and put onto waxed paper.

Chocolate Divinity

3 cups sugar
½ cup water
⅓ cup white corn syrup
2 egg whites
½ cup walnut meats, chopped
1 teaspoon vanilla
5 squares semi-sweet
    chocolate, cut in pieces

Combine sugar, water and syrup in a saucepan. Cook without stirring to 250° F. or until a small amount of mixture forms a hard ball in cold water. Beat egg whites until stiff, and pour syrup in a fine stream over egg whites and beat until mixture begins to thicken or stiffen. Add nut meats, vanilla and chocolate. Drop from teaspoons onto a waxed paper and cool thoroughly.

Gramma Lloyd's Divinity Fudge

2 cups sugar
½ cup light corn syrup
2 egg whites
½ cup water
1 teaspoon vanilla
¼ teaspoon salt
⅓ cup chopped nuts

Boil sugar, syrup and water without stirring until a firm ball forms when dropped in cold water. Pour at once into stiffly beaten egg whites. Beat until stiff and dull. Add vanilla, salt and chopped nuts. Pour into buttered shallow pan. Cool and cut when firm or drop by teaspoons onto waxed paper.

Hershey's Cocoa Fudge

⅔ cup Hershey's cocoa
3 cups sugar
⅛ teaspoon salt
1 large can carnation milk
¼ cup butter
1 tablespoon vanilla
⅔ cup chopped walnuts

Combine thoroughly the dry ingredients in a heavy cast iron skillet. Bring to a boil over medium heat, stirring constantly. Boil without stirring to 234° F. (or soft ball stage when dropped into cold water). Remove from heat. Stir in butter, vanilla and walnuts. Beat until it loses its gloss. Pour into an 8x8 buttered dish. Cool. Cut into squares.

Peanut Butter Fudge

Same as Hershey's cocoa fudge; just omit the chopped walnuts and add ⅔ cup of Jiff creamy peanut butter.

Grandmother Lloyd's Vinegar Taffy

1 cup sugar
¼ cup light corn syrup
¼ teaspoon soda
1 teaspoon vinegar
½ cup boiling water
½ teaspoon flavor

Boil sugar, syrup, water and vinegar without stirring until a firm or thick ball forms when added to cold water. Add soda and flavoring. Pour into a buttered dish. When cool enough to handle, pull until crisp.

Hot Buttered Rum Batter

1 pound dark brown sugar
½ pound soft butter
1½ teaspoons cloves
(or more to taste)
1½ teaspoons cinnamon
1½ teaspoons nutmeg

Mix together well. Cover and refrigerate. Use a walnut size lump for each cup of water mixed with 1½ jigger of dark rum.

Mrs. Brogan's Tom And Jerry Batter

Mrs. Brogan used to make this Tom and Jerry Batter every July 25th for Christmas in Idaho City, Idaho. When there was a Smoke Jumper Base in Idaho City, Idaho, Christmas was always celebrated on the 25th of July. Presents were exchanged and Christmas carols were sung from Mrs. Brogan's horse and buggy. Jack Williams used to go up in his plane and play carols from up above the city. Always a good time was had by all.

12 fresh eggs
½ small bar glass of
 Jamaica Rum
1½ teaspoons cinnamon
½ teaspoon cloves
½ teaspoon allspice
Sufficient sugar
 (Bar sugar - see note)

Beat the whites of eggs to a stiff froth; add the yolks which have been beaten until thin, and mix. Add the spices and rum, stir thoroughly and thicken with sugar to the consistency of a light batter.

Also add 1 tablespoon cream of tarter or a small pinch of soda to prevent sugar from settling. (cream of tarter is the best). To mix: 1 tablespoon batter, one wine glass of brandy. Fill mug with boiling water and sprinkle with nutmeg. Serve with a spoon. Or: substitute mixture of ½ brandy, ½ Jamaica rum, ½ Santa Cruz Rum.

Note: Use superfine sugar.

Egg Nog

To Serve 12

12 egg yolks
½ cup superfine sugar
1 fifth of Black Jack
Daniels whiskey
1½ cups dark Barcardi Rum
2 cups milk
1 quart of heavy cream, chilled
The whites of the 12 eggs
1 tablespoon nutmeg

In a large bowl beat the egg yolks and sugar together with an egg beater until the mixture is thick enough to fall back on itself in a slow ribbon. With a wooden spoon beat in the whiskey, rum and milk. Cover the bowl with plastic wrap and refrigerate overnight.

Just before serving the egg nog, whip the cream until stiff enough to hold strong peaks when the mixer is lifted from the bowl. Beat the egg whites in a separate bowl until they hold up in stiff peaks. Now fold the whipped cream into the egg white mixture, be sure to fold lightly with a rubber spatula. Pour the egg yolk mixture into a large punch bowl, add the egg-white mixture and fold gently until there is no trace of the whites. Sprinkle with the nutmeg. Serve at once from chilled punch cups.

On a cold winter night, a fire in the fireplace and guests coming for dinner or a card game, this is one recipe that will warm all your hearts.

Homemade Lemonade

2 cups sugar
2 cups water
12 large lemons
2½ to 3 quarts
of cold water

Prepare a simple syrup by boiling together the sugar and 2 cups water. As soon as the syrup is clear and smooth set aside to cool. Juice the lemons (you shoud have about 2 cups). Pour lemon juice in gallon container. Add cold water in a ratio of 5 to 6 to 1 (10 to 12 cups water to 2 cups lemon juice). Add 1 cup of the syrup to mixture. Stir and taste; add more water and/or more syrup if needed. Makes 1 gallon.

As a young girl, I remember sitting on the front steps and rolling lemons until they were soft – and mother making 5 gallons of this lemonade to take out to the fields to the thrashing crews.

Vanilla Ice Cream

2 pints of ½ and ½
3 four-inch vanilla beans
1½ cups sugar
3 eggs
1 tablespoon vanilla
6 cups heavy whipping cream
¼ cup rum
Chopped ice
Rock salt

In a saucepan heat until small bubbles form the 2 pints of ½ and ½ and the vanilla beans. Let stand until cool. Take out the vanilla beans. Cut the vanilla beans, scrape out the seeds, put the seeds into the ½ and ½. Mix together the sugar, 3 eggs, slightly beaten, 1 tablespoon vanilla, add to the ½ and ½. Stir well. Add this to the 6 cups of heavy cream. Add the rum. Put into freezer and churn until the handle is hard to turn.

Rum Vanilla Ice Cream

2 cups ½ and ½
2 vanilla beans
1¾ cups sugar

Heat in saucepan until warm the 2 cups ½ and ½, vanilla beans and 1¾ cups sugar.

Add 3 eggs, slightly beaten. Remove from heat. Scrape seeds from vanilla beans. Add seeds back to mixture.

Add:

3 more cups ½ and ½
2 cups milk
3½ pints of heavy whipping cream
¼ cup rum
½ teaspoon salt

Mix well and pour into the freezer pan. Pack with rock salt and ice. Churn until handle is stiff to turn.

Vanilla Ice Cream

1½ cups sugar
3 eggs
3 cups milk
2 tablespoons vanilla
¼ teaspoon salt
3 cups cream

Blend everything together and put into freezer. Churn with rock salt and chopped ice until freezer handle is tight to turn.

To make a larger batch of vanilla ice cream add 2 cups ½ and ½ and put in an additional 1 cup of cream.

Also, vanilla bean can be substituted for the vanilla.

Pickles

Pickled Beets

Select small young beets. Cook until tender and peel.

Mix together:
2 cups sugar
2 cups water
2 cups strong vinegar
1 teaspoon cloves
1 teaspoon allspice
1 tablespoon cinnamon

Pour syrup over beets and boil 10 minutes. Put into sterilized jars and seal.

Grandma Lloyd's Dill Pickles

2 quarts water
1 quart vinegar
1 cup salt
alum
dill
cucumbers

Mix water, vinegar and salt together. Bring to a boil. Pour over cucumbers that have been packed into sterilized jars, with a head of dill on the bottom and place a head of dill on top. Add a teaspoon of alum on top. Cover and seal at once. May be deep water bathed for 10 minutes. You may also add a small red pepper and a clove of garlic. Garlic should be boiled for 5 minutes before being added to pickles.

Jalapeño Pepper Jelly

2 large green peppers
8 jalapeño peppers (chopped) fresh jalapeño peppers are to be used. You may add or subtract due to your taste.
1½ cups vinegar
5½ cups sugar
1 6-oz. bottle Certo or 2 packs
Few drops green food coloring (optional)

Chop green and hot peppers, put ½ cup peppers and ½ cup vinegar in blender, put in large pan. Put remaining peppers and ½ cup vinegar in blender. Blend, then pour into pan with other peppers and vinegar. Put ½ cup vinegar in blender to clean — then pour into pan with rest of peppers. Stir in sugar. Bring to a full rolling boil that you cannot stir down. Boil 1 minute. Remove from heat, skim, add green food coloring. Pour in and stir well the one bottle of Certo.

Let stand 5 minutes. Skim and pour into sterilized jars and seal.

Makes 8 6-oz. jars.

Sweet Pickle Sticks

Wash and cut into sticks 20 to 30 cucumbers.
Pour boiling water over them and let stand for 4 to 5 hours.
Weigh them down with a plate. Drain and pack into sterilized pint jars.

Brine:

3¾ cups vinegar
3 cups sugar
3 tablespoons pickling salt
4½ teaspoons celery seed
¾ teaspoons mustard seed
4½ teaspoons tumeric

Put all ingredients together in a pan and bring to a boil. Boil for 5 minutes. Pour over packed cucumbers. Seal. Deep water bath for 5 minutes.

My Mom's Crisp Watermelon Pickles

Use rind of one large melon; cut off green and pink meat. Cut into strips about 1½ inch long and 1 inch wide. Soak in 1 gallon of water with 2 tablespoons salt for 12 hours. Rinse and let stand for 1 hour in ice water. Drain and cover with boiling water. Put in kettle and cook and simmer until tender enough to pierce with a toothpick. Drain and drop into hot syrup.

Syrup:
7 cups granulated sugar
2 cups fine cider vinegar
1 tablespoon whole cloves
3 sticks cinnamon

Put into a large pan and cook slowly until clear. Then add melon rinds and cook until melon is transparent. Be sure not to over cook the melon.

Let set for 24 hours.

Pack melon into sterile jars. Heat syrup and pour over melon rinds. Seal jars.

Be sure to have jars and lids hot.

Grandma Lloyd's Piccalilli

½ gallon chopped cabbage
1 quart chopped onion
4 sweet red peppers
4 green bell peppers
1 quart green tomatoes, ground

Grind first five ingredients together.

Sprinkle the above with salt and let stand overnight. Drain off liquid and put into kettle with:

2 cups sugar
1 teaspoon cinnamon
1 teaspoon cloves
½ teaspoon allspice
enough vinegar to cover

Boil 15 minutes. Put into sterilized jars and seal.

Green Tomato Relish

12 medium onions
(4 cups ground)
1 medium or 2 small heads
cabbage (4 cups ground)
12 green tomatoes or
4 cups ground
4 sweet red bell peppers, ground
½ cup salt
6 cups sugar
2 tablespoons mustard seed
1 tablespoon celery seed
1½ teaspoons turmeric
4 cups cider vinegar
2 cups water

Grind vegetables, using a coarse blade. Put into a large bowl; sprinkle with salt; cover and let set overnight.

Next morning rinse and drain. Put into a large pan. Combine all remaining ingredients, sugar, mustard seed, celery seed, turmeric, vinegar and water. Pour over vegetables. Heat to boiling. Simmer three minutes. Seal in hot sterilized jars. Makes 8 pints.

Pat's Hot Dill Pickles

40 lbs. of small 3 inch or 4 inch cucumbers
Approximately 30 fresh grape leaves (washed)
Dill (fresh or dried may be used)
garlic, enough for one clove per quart, (garlic should be boiled for 10 minutes)
dried or fresh red hot peppers, one per quart
1 teaspoon mustard seed per quart
30 jalapeno type fresh green peppers

For Brine: 3 quarts of water,1 quart vinegar, 1 cup salt.

Bring to a rapid boil. Pour over cucumbers that have been packed into clean hot sterilized jars. Pack as follows: one grape leave in bottom of each jar, one large dill head, then pack cucumbers, hot red pepper, jalapeno pepper, garlic, (small onion may be added) add the teaspoon of mustard seed. One large dill head on top. Pour the brine over the top to ½ inch of rim. Seal with lids that have been setting in boiling water. Process for 10 minutes in hot water bath.

Continue making brine as needed.

Note: The fresh grape leaves are what makes these pickles firm. *Do not omit them or substitute alum.*

All pickles have a shelf life, before eating. These are not ready to eat for at least 6 weeks to 2 months. But are well worth the wait.

Gramma Lloyd's Rhubarb Wine

Wash rhubarb good. Cut in 1-inch pieces. Put into stone jar and for each pound of rhubarb, pour one quart of boiling water. Let stand for 3 days. Stir each day. Then strain through cloth, squeezing rhubarb a little. Then for each gallon of juice add 3 pounds of white sugar, 1 cup raisins, 1 lemon sliced and 1 orange sliced. Let stand for 9 days, stirring each day (keep in a warm place). Then strain and put in keg or bottles, but do not cap tight for about 3 weeks to a month. In about 2 months wine should be good to drink.

Home Canned Tomatoes

Select fresh, vine ripe, firm unblemished tomatoes. Bring to a boil a pot of water. Pour over tomatoes and let set for 1 minute; rinse with cold water to loosen skins. Drain. Remove skins and core. Leave tomatoes whole or quarter, as desired. Pack into hot clean, sterilized jars. Pack tight and to within ½ inch from top of jar. Add 1 teaspoon of canning salt to each quart and ½ teaspoon of canning salt to each pint.

Top with lids that have been heated in a pan of hot water. Tighten rings nice and tight.

Process at 5 pounds of pressure for 10 minutes in your pressure cooker.

For the deep water method, cover with an inch of water and boil for 45 minutes. Add more water as needed to keep jars covered.

Note: ½ bushel of tomatoes will put up approximately 10 quarts of tomatoes.

Note: Use 5 pounds of pressure, for 10 minutes when at 2,000 feet elevation. Increase pressure to 10 pounds when at 5,000 feet elevation.

Home Canned Rum Applebutter

Choose tart or wine sap apples
¼ bushel of apples or enough to make
8 cups of pulp
For applebutter:
8 cups pulp from apples
2 cups dark brown sugar
2 cups white granulated sugar
1 tablespoon cinnamon
1½ teaspoons cloves
½ teaspoon allspice
Juice from 1 lemon
½ cup dark Barcardi rum

Cut stem from apples and wash off blossoms. Cut apples into quarters. Put into a large pan or roasting pan. Add enough water or apple juice to almost cover. Cook on low heat on top of stove until apples are soft and mushy. Add more water or apple juice as needed to keep apples from sticking. This will take an hour or more. When apples are soft, remove from stove and run through a wire strainer. Toss away seeds and pulp. Measure 8 cups of pulp and put into large roaster pan. Add brown sugar, white sugar, spices, lemon juice and rum. Put into oven set at 300° F. Cook stirring every one-half hour, to keep from sticking. Cook until mixture coats a stainless steel spoon. It take three hours or more. When thickened, put into hot sterilized jars and seal. Be sure that your lids have been boiled in hot water to insure that the jars seal. Makes 4 pints. Approximately 33 calories per tablespoon.

INDEX

FAVORITE RECIPES